Pumpkin Seed Point

Being Within the Hopi

OTHER BOOKS BY FRANK WATERS

Pumpkin Seed Point
Being Within the Hopi

Frank Waters

SAGE BOOKS

SWALLOW PRESS
ATHENS

Reprinted in 1981, 1985, 1989 by Ohio University Press

Sage/Swallow Press Books
are published by
Ohio University Press

ISBN 0-8040-0635-0 (Paper)

Library of Congress Catalog Number 76-75741

Swallow Press/Ohio University Press books are printed on acid-free paper. ∞

ACKNOWLEDGMENTS

The essence of Chapter 6 was delivered as a talk at the Fourth Annual Arizona Historical Convention, sponsored by the University of Arizona and the Arizona Pioneers' Historical Society, in Tucson, Arizona, in March 1963; and was published in the May 1964 issue of *The South Dakota Review*.

Portions of Chapters 9 and 10 were delivered as the third writer-in-residence lecture sponsored by the Fine Arts Series of the Colorado State University, Fort Collins, Colorado, in January 1966; and was published by the Fine Arts Series under the title *Mysticism and Witchcraft*.

Thanks are given to both publications for permission to include the material here.

The full objective report on the Hopis, which is referred to in this personal, subjective narrative, was made for the Charles Ulrick and Josephine Bay Foundation, New York; and was published by The Viking Press, New York, under the title *Book of the Hopi*.

Illustrations on pages 1, 14, 26, 55, 86, 100, 111, 127, 140 by Alfred Young; on pages 63, 74, 157, 168 by L. Miller.
Cover and Book Design by L. Miller and V. Seper/Chicago

for SUSIE

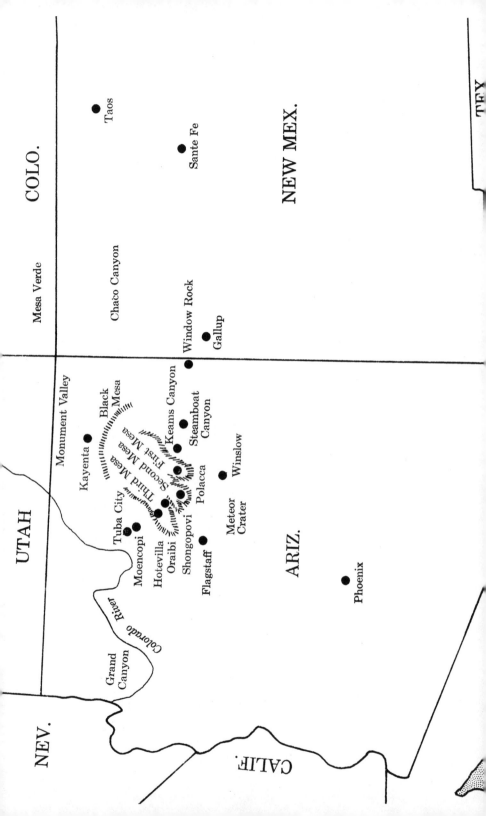

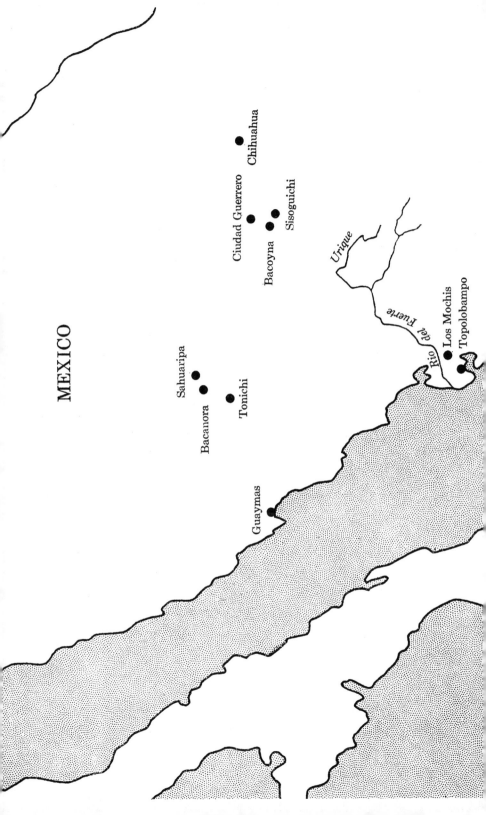

TABLE OF CONTENTS

FOREWORD

Not long ago, after a lifelong association with American Indians, I spent the greater part of three years living among the Hopis in northern Arizona, the strangest, most secretive and obdurate tribe left in the United States. The purpose of my stay was to record from a number of wrinkled old spokesmen their traditional religious beliefs and instinctive perception of life processes which our rationally extroverted white observers still ignore to the impoverishment of our mechanistic-materialistic civilization. During this time I also made two trips down among the Tarahumaras in the Sierra Madre of Chihuahua, the most remote, primitive, and least-known tribe in Mexico.

The present book is a personal narrative of my inner and outer experiences in this subterranean world of Indian America. Its surface extent remains unchanged from ancient times—that vast motherland stretching southward from the mesas of New Mexico and Arizona through the plateaus of Mexico to the jungles of Yucatan, dotted by prehistoric ruins such as those of Chaco Canyon, Casas Grandes, majestic Teotihuacan, and the sublime Mayan pyramid-temple cities; and still populated by dozens of tribes once embraced within the Toltec-Aztec-Mayan complex. Over it now, since the Conquest, has spread the veneer of Spanish and Anglo-European dominance with its proud superstructures of rational thought. Underground it remains the same. An immense tract of indigenous people—of Tarahumaras hiding in the abysmal depths of their mighty *barrancas* and of Hopis isolating themselves on the island tips of their lofty desert mesas, in countless pueblos and Reservations on sunstruck plains and desolate deserts, and in *barrios* of impoverished people in the slum districts of all large cities—all still attuned to the instinctual and intuitional polarity of their primeval, uniquely American past.

Little wonder that we whites, with our desperate reliance upon

surface physical reality, seldom perceive that in this Indian sub-
stream lies an America we have never known, yet embodying the
truths of our own unconscious, the repressed elements of our darker,
deeper selves. It was not enough for us here in the United States
to almost exterminate the red race in our sweep across the continent. Its ghosts still walk the land, and in our unconscious the
Indian is a potent symbol.

During my work, a number of strange things happened that
revealed the hidden, obverse side of the picture. In the depths of
the Indian soul there lie a mistrust and a hatred of whites unresolved by his expanding consciousness. Current government aid,
tourist pampering, and false sentimentality reflect how heavy Indians lie on our conscience, but they also project on us the darker
aspect of their own dual nature. Against the evil which we represent, they erect the bulwark of the exclusive divinity of their own
literally believed myths whose transcendent meaning has never risen
to conscious recognition. They are a people driven to secrecy and
aloofness by their sense of inferiority as an impoverished minority,
by a messianic compulsion that compensates for their loss of land
and birthright.

So we find ourselves at this great verge, the red and the white,
two brothers of a common humanity held apart by two opposite
complementary principles which neither of us has reconciled.

It is so easy to generalize, to talk in terms of races and nations. But we cannot ignore the cracks in the volcanic floor of
Mexico through which are re-emerging in art and architecture,
music and social reforms, the Indian values of the ancient past. Yet
reconciliation of the opposites, the assimilation of the contents of
the unconscious into consciousness, cannot be achieved by the
mass. The mass is made up of individuals and it is in the individual,
both red and white, where the conflict must be resolved.

This book is an account of the conflict at close quarters, within myself and within my Hopi associates, and between us, on a level far below our surface covenants and quarrels. It is a rereading of old myths, old dreams in universal terms. Indeed, as I look back to those tortuous, lonely years spent beneath the craggy cliffs of Pumpkin Seed Point, it seems that we were re-enacting again those spiritual myth-dramas of ancient America whose meanings must some day be plain to us all.

1. THE HOUSE AT PUMPKIN SEED POINT

It was a long walk home to the little house just below Pumpkin Seed Point. The distance wasn't far, scarcely a half mile. What made it seem long was the cold and the snow, darkness and silence. The acrid cold ate like a corrosive through the woolen scarf wrapped around my ears. The snow covering the rutted dirt road was frozen hard. Every step squeaked shrilly in the silence. Under the gritty winter stars the earth spread out flat and bare, save for the jagged, rocky mesa jutting forth at Pumpkin Seed Point.

In the faint luminous starlight a small stone building emerged in empty space. The post office. Farther off, the white clapboard Mennonite mission church loomed up, a pale ghost shunned even on Sunday by all but a few converts. To its right squatted the low, sprawling trading post. It was an island in a sea of frozen mud covered with snow. A naked electric light bulb glared through its iron-barred windows, and there sounded the putt-putt-putt of the coughing gasoline engine that generated its juice. They were the only light and sound in this modern Hopi village of Kiakochomovi, which we know as New Oraibi.

Beyond and behind the trading post I trudged past most of the houses in town. Sturdy little buildings of stone hewn from the rocky mesas, a few plastered over with adobe. Others mere hovels set into the side of the hill rising below Pumpkin Seed Point. They all had been dark and lifeless since eight o'clock. Even the gaunt Indian dogs lay quiet and shivering in front of the doors barred against witches.

The hill was not high, but it was a problem in all weathers. During spring and summer rains it was slippery with thick mud. It was worse when covered with winter's snow and ice. Most of the time you abandoned your car at the bottom and walked up. There mine stood now, securely locked against stray Navajos, its windshield covered with ice.

THE HOUSE AT PUMPKIN SEED POINT

Slipping and panting now, I reached the top of the hill. To the left, backed against the rocky slope of Pumpkin Seed Point, huddled a cluster of houses. In front of it to the right lay a huge pile of firewood that supplied many of the families. This was desert country and the great logs had been brought from mountains as far away as a hundred miles. Most of them were cedar or juniper, for cedar splits easily and burns fast. It is no good for fireplaces: it throws out too many sparks. But the Hopis couldn't afford fireplaces, and they conserved every splinter to burn in their cooking stoves. So all day long, every day, you would see men hacking away at these great, twisted tree trunks, and women and children patiently gathering up chips and splinters.

This hilltop was a focal point of life for more than the woodpile. It was also Crier's Point, for here the Village Crier stood to cry out important news and announcements. Somehow he always chose early morning for the chore. You were blasted out of bed by his guttural, singsong voice. Rushing to the window, you saw this devil's advocate, one foot propped up on the woodpile, shouting into space. Hopi is a voluble language; it took him five minutes or more to inform the waiting world of momentous news. What it had been this morning, paradoxically, was the announcement that the *Independent* of Gallup, New Mexico, was now starting to deliver newspapers to the Reservation for the first time. This step in progress, it is unnecessary to prophecy, would go unheeded. It was easier to listen to the Crier Chief.

How lonely it was to stand here in the freezing cold, seeing only the reflection of that one light and listening to that putt-putt below, the only light and sound. There wasn't much else to notice. Only the high spur of Third Mesa to the west, on which lay the original Old Oraibi. The oldest continually inhabited settlement in the United States, it was an archaeological ruin of falling walls still populated by less than a hundred people. Below it a dimly marked dirt road crawled south to Winslow, a hundred miles away, the closest town. Nobody took it. It was easier to cross the desert to the west, then drive south to Flagstaff, 125 miles away. Or to drive east, past Second and First Mesa, to Gallup, New Mexico, 130 miles away. How desolate and empty! The snowy sage-plain spread out as far as one could see. Here from a tiny hilltop on the high plateau of northern Arizona, here in the ancient, wilderness heartland of an America we have never known.

Man must have much of the wild animal in him yet. Or perhaps I am one who had slept out too much, and for too many years, to crawl into his lair without a look around. Nor can I enter a strange house for the first time without peeking out all windows to orient myself to the directions. So I stood here every night for a moment before going inside.

Perhaps for a look at the stars. Nowhere else do they glitter so nakedly bright, nor seem so intimately close to their faint reflection in the crystalline snow. There was the great, immortal pattern of Orion with *Hotomkan,* the highest star in his belt, sparkling clear. Above it the cluster of the Pleiades, which the Hopis call *Choochhokam,* the Harmonious Ones, the Stars That Cling Together. And below it *Ponochona,* the One Who Sucks From the Belly, the star that controls the lives of all beings in the animal kingdom. These and millions more in constellations and galactic clusters were spread lavishly as snow across the plain of the sky above.

White Bear and I were particularly interested in these stars, for their winter patterns and movements guided the timing of the sacred songs and rituals for the Hopi priests who watched them through the roof openings of their underground kivas. These great ceremonies were now in progress. At that very moment naked, painted men in a dozen kivas in nine mesa-top villages nearby were watching and praying to these stars for guidance. Tawdry villages they were, their crooked streets and cramped plazas littered with refuse and ordure. But villages still consecrated to their ancient faith. The thought somehow lent life to the darkness and silence, the desolate emptiness of the starlit landscape.

Our own people, our own white race, have long used these same stars to guide our physical selves across illimitable plains and seas. We are still using them in our first crude voyages into space. But few among us ever deign now to use them for guidance of our inner selves. We've proudly outgrown that nonsense, thank you. How sad! How dreary really to so stifle the whispers of our intuitive selves.

But then I, like many others, owe allegiance not to one race and people, but to two. One part of me is inherently attuned to that masculine, mental, Euro-American world whose monuments of rational materialism rise higher and higher every year. The other part of me is forever polarized to the feminine realm of instinct, the dark unconscious. Thus, every so often I find myself helplessly drawn back into still-living, ancient America; into the sub-world of continental Indian America; into the Hopi village of New Oraibi, immune, as it always has been, to change and progress.

My little house, its stone walls freshly plastered with adobe, was one of several in the group. Between the houses ran a *zaguan*, a narrow alley, to the lower rocky slope of Pumpkin Seed Point. Here, upright among great boulders, stood the decrepit wooden outhouses. Formerly here, as at all Hopi villages, a little ledge of rock was reserved for each family's use. Now with progress had come a rash of privies on the rocky slopes. The trail to these was deep with snow and it was unbroken. It was easier and more customary to dash outside and squat in the blue shadows of the house walls. The custom did not add to the imagined picturesqueness of the Hopi villages, so choked with refuse and human offal. But it drove home a jutting fact of life: that out of a garbage heap, a pile of manure, often grows the most beautiful flower. And this flower grown from Hopi poverty and dirt was the kachina, an art form unequalled anywhere else in the world; a flower of faith such as we have not been able to grow out of our antiseptic culture pot. The kachina was a masked human figure, an anthropomorphic image of the spirit of life. There were as many kachinas as there were forms of life—vegetable, animal, man, and star. You could see them all, a hundred and more, during the Páchavu ceremony, when from all directions they came dancing into the plaza; each one differently masked in his own unearthly shape, each uttering his own strange cry. How strangely compelling and wonderful they were!

Where they all came from, God only knew. They seemed to come from distant stars, or to spring from myth and the earth itself. One of them manifested herself at high noon here on Pumpkin Seed Point before going to the plaza. She was Héhewúti, the Warrior Mother. On her black mask were painted two great yellow eyes with black pupils, and a rectangular mouth edged with red and showing her bared teeth. From it protruded her long red tongue. Her hair was done up in a whorl on one side and hung full length on the other. She wore a black loomed dress secured at the waist with a long fringed sash, over which was draped a black cape. Over her shoulder was hung a buckskin quiver full of arrows. In her left hand she carried a bow, in her right a rattle.

Héhewúti was a mythical figure who lived far to the south, maybe in Central or South America, in the mysterious red city of Palátkwapi. On the morning when it was attacked and destroyed by enemies, Héhewúti was putting up her hair. That is

5

why her hair was done up on one side but still hung loose on the other. Immediately she threw on her clothes, which is why she still looks so untidy, and grabbed up her bow and quiver to help defend the city. Now on the day of Páchavu she stood on Pumpkin Seed Point, singing a song which echoed the cries of her people in their distress. The same song still sung by natives in Central America, according to some visiting missionaries. Whatever her meaning, Héhewúti, frightening, strange, and untidy, somehow expressed the feeling of Pumpkin Seed Point.

How damnable cold it was!

But the key to my little house was waiting under the stone beside the door, and the beam of a flashlight guided it into the lock.

The first spurt of the gaslight illuminated the room. In one corner was a small butane gas stove. From this ran a small pipe to a gaslight fixture mounted on the wall above the bed in the opposite corner. Its location was awkward. The light was not bright enough to work by at the table against the window. Nor was the kerosene lamp I brought with me when I moved in. So by necessity I worked at the table by daylight, and wrote up my notes in bed at night. There were two other pieces of furniture in the room: a dresser in the far dark corner and a spare chair.

There were two other smaller rooms in the house, both unlighted and unused, and closed off by blankets hung over the doorways to keep out the cold. The room at the far end contained an unmade bed, a sagging Montgomery-Ward's clothes closet, a jumbled disarray of boxes and suitcases, and a bag of golf clubs. "Pneumonia's Boudoir," the Professor called it when he came for a visit.

The room at the other end was just as dark and dreary. It contained an old iron cooking stove whose stovepipe was unconnected, and a table on which were set a bucket of water and a washbasin. On the floor beneath it was a white enamel chamber pot, as well as all the glass bottles and thermos jugs in which I brought water from the spring at Hotevilla, ten miles away. Here in the cold darkness I washed hurriedly and came back to stand shivering for a moment beside the gas stove before jumping into bed. How pleasant it was to lie here, knees propped up, notebooks and cigarettes on the chair beside me, in this room which was my home over a period of nearly three years. What makes a room congenial is an intangible quality that cannot be planned for in advance. You can't prescribe its correct proportions, nor can you build in congeniality with interior decoration and furnishings.

Up in Taos, New Mexico, where my own home was, Indians and Mexicans achieved charm with simplicity. The clay-washed adobe walls were never laid with a plumb-line. The floors were of hard-beaten earth. A conical Indian fireplace was built into the corner, and the roof beams were great honey-smooth spruce logs interlaced with small, straight aspen poles.

The simplicity of this Hopi room lacked such elements of charm. The walls were bare and whitewashed. There were cracks between the floor boards. The roof beams were crooked, ill-matched, and whitewashed too. One of them was a large knotted joint tapering off at both ends. It looked like a broken knee in a plaster cast. Over them were laced willow branches which supported a thick roof of mud to keep out rain and snow. There was no fireplace to give life to the room. And there were no pictures. Only a few kachina dolls hanging on the wall, and several clumps of small eagle feathers dangling from the ceiling. These were prayer-feathers or *pahos* made for me, each a prayer.

Still this bare little room gave forth an atmosphere of comfort and peace and contentment to which I was always glad to return after every absence. Despite its cozy atmosphere one always noticed its faint odor immediately upon entering. A rather acrid smell that permeated not only this house, but all the houses of every Hopi village, the earth itself.

The Professor when he came detected it at once. It bothered him because he could not ascertain what caused it. He decided it could not come from the water, for the springs on all three mesas were free of the smell. Perhaps, he conjectured, it came from the refuse and ordure that littered the ground. This I rejected. The faint odor of urine-soaked earth was Mexico's distinctive smell; every little village was permeated with it. Nor was this smell a typical Indian smell, for I had never noticed it in any of the other Indian pueblos in Arizona and New Mexico.

The Professor went away still perplexed, charging me to run down its cause. I have not yet been able to oblige him. For quite possibly this was uniquely Hopi, a tribal or racial odor that for nine centuries or more had charged every building, every village, the earth itself, with the olfactory vibration of their mysterious uniqueness. At any rate, it was not disagreeable and one soon accepted it with everything else Hopi—with the tranquility of this little house itself that nothing seemed to disturb.

It seemed strange to me, the night I first moved in, to be warned to lock the door at night.

"I don't mind the neighbors peeking in the windows. They'll soon get use to me," I answered. "Stray Navajos won't break in, either. They steal only what's left outside."

White Bear shook his head.

"You don't think any Hopis will object so much to what we're doing that they'll come to make a fuss, do you?"

White Bear shook his head more solemnly. "I have been

warned to tell you that if you are in earnest, you will have a manifestation of some kind to prove your sincerity. That might frighten you. So lock the door."

It seemed odd to me then that a mere locked door would keep out either a witch or a good spirit if it chose to enter, but White Bear refused to say more. But that night, long after midnight, I was suddenly awakened by a noise that sounded like gravel being thrown against the window pane. I lay stiffly in bed until there sounded another loud splatter against the glass. Then I jumped up and flung open the door. No one, nothing was there. The hilltop, all the village, was dark and silent. There was only the reflection of that bare globe in the trading post and the putt-putt-putt of its coughing engine.

After that, nothing of the sort seemed strange at all. Other things occurred, over and over, inexplicable perhaps but not frightening. Even then, that first night, I somehow felt that here I was confronting what might be an added dimension to the life we normally lead in our highly mental and materialistic civilization so far removed in time and space from this still-living, ancient, heartland of a dwindling remnant of another race. I do not mean to imply that the Hopis had a monopoly on witches and spirits; our overcrowded mental institutions attest to the invisible forces that plague us also. Rather that their beneficent and inimical images assumed different forms, for they all are created alike by our own minds to manifest our secret fears and desires.

So I lay here in bed, knees up, scrawling in a stenographer's notebook with a blunt copy pencil my nightly notes. If they seemed to accentuate the differences between the Hopis and us, it is only because we are two sides of the same coin. I kept reminding myself that it was a room in New York which launched me to this room in New Oraibi.

I recalled it vividly and pleasantly. It was in the Wall Street skyscraper that housed the New York Stock Exchange. Nowhere in the world save on the lower tip of Manhattan Island—not even in postcard Arizona—rises such a fantastic growth of lofty buttes, dizzy stone pillars, and needlepoint crags from a maze of dark canyons and sunless gorges swarming with toiling ants. This directors' room on the eighteenth floor seemed comfortably isolated from all signs of labor. You could, if you wished, be quickly conducted to the Pit for a peep at the saturnalia of shouting men and streamers of ticker tape that controlled the national industry, international trade, and the price of a bag of flour in the trading post at New Oraibi. But it was more pleasant to sit on the long couch in front of the massive directors' table and look at the view.

There were two views in the room.

The magnificent wallpaper gave a nostalgic view of sailing ships docking at the wharves below, long before other white-sheeted schooners rolled westward over the pelagic plain to find the remote and isolated Hopis obstructing the course of empire. The window gave a contemporary view of the same scene: the great liner *Queen Mary* being tugged upriver to her dock.

These two views were separated in space only by the width of a window frame, but in time by a century and a half. During that long span the rolling sweep of conquest had caught up with the Hopis, engulfing them in riptides of military domination, government control, and racial discrimination. Then it had spewed them out again—a rejected handful of people clinging to nine crumbling villages on the high summits of three mesas a hundred miles or more from the nearest transcontinental highway.

There were several persons in the room, all dominated by a single woman wearing a long mink coat and sitting in the director's seat at the table. "The First Lady of Wall Street," as reporters

10

often called her, was middle-aged, with a commanding presence and sharp eyes; a woman of considerable importance whose business acumen was respected in many fields. Yet this only threw into sharper relief the kindness and understanding that infused her whole personality.

The spokesman of the group was a tall, lanky man who knew what he was talking about. He put it briefly. The group wanted to help the Hopis. Not by making an academic study of them and their present difficulties—neither an ethnological or economic report, nor a sociological or psychological paper, to be filed away in museums and libraries—but by persuading them to relate freely, for the first time, the complete history and religious beliefs of their people. This, it was hoped, would provide both a basis for understanding their current problems and a permanent record of their traditions for their children and their children's children.

"We ourselves desire to remain anonymous, although charitable funds made possible by this Foundation will provide financial support for the effort," he concluded. "Does this summarize our discussion and correctly state our position?" he asked the other directors.

It was that fabulous, that simple, really. A manifestation of national conscience in a Wall Street brokerage office? An Angel with a seat on the New York Stock Exchange unfolding wings over the forgotten Hopis?

The project appealed to me from the start. All my life I had known Indians and had written much about them, and I felt I now owed them some constructive help in return for all they had given me. Perhaps this was merely a rational excuse for doing still another book on those neglected people who, despite my efforts to break away from the mold of their thought, had always drawn me back with an incomprehensible fascination. This was an un-

11

usual challenge. It involved obtaining from the Hopis, secretive as they were, their complete Creation myth, the legends of their prehistoric migrations over this continent, the esoteric meanings of their religious ceremonies, and their own view of historical events since the coming of the white man—the first full record, to my knowledge, of an Indian tribe from its own uncontested viewpoint.

As my work progressed, it kept throwing into focus many incompletely realized things I had felt about other Indians. The Hopis, unique as they were, seemed to be speaking not only for their race but for all primitive peoples who still preserved the ancestral myths and archetypal images which linked them with the nurturing unconscious. At the same time, it kept throwing into new perspective a strange Euro-America perversely strangling itself with its excessive rationality and materialism, the specter of modern civilization.

Yet, enriching as this was, I found myself ever so often rebelling against the Hopis' obdurate aloofness, their needless squalor, lack of initiative, and illogical prejudices—everything that characterized them as Indian. An overpowering compulsion urged me to get away for awhile. There is always a great danger in developing too great an empathy with a primitive people. For consciousness evolves out of the unconscious just as the physical body evolves from primeval anatomical forms; and despite the exhortations of D. H. Lawrence and his cult, we can't go back.

But we whites, I felt, were succumbing to the greater danger of closing off, with the rationalizations of our limited conscious minds, the images and urges of the boundless unconscious which fed life itself. So again I returned to New Oraibi to feel the Hopis' archaic closeness to the wonder and the mystery and the sense of wholeness that stemmed from it.

This polarity of opposite dualities I found was the basic difference between Indian America and Euro-America, between the Hopis and ourselves. It was also the schism that divided each one of us internally. I discovered that every Hopi in some measure, like myself, was two persons: an outer man consciously confronted with the problems of existence in a swiftly changing, material world; and an inner man attuned to the greater realm of the unconscious, the matrix of all creation.

Over and over again, as my work developed surface differences between the United States and the Hopi Empire, as this staunchly independent little tribe pathetically called itself, I saw the same differences reflected on a vaster scale by rival world powers. These differences would not be reconciled on the expedient level of politics, economics, and the threat of war. They could only be resolved by tearing down the Iron Curtain that divided our inner selves.

So here at Pumpkin Seed Point I lay in bed after work each night scribbling notes about the two peoples who objectified the conflicting forces of my own nature and illumined my quest of self-discovery. Personal notes and anecdotes about the Hopis who projected their fears and prejudices on the whites who for so long have projected their own fears and prejudices on all Indians. Two invisible projections clashing in the air. Which one had thrown gravel against my window pane? Perhaps, after all, I had better get up and throw the catch on the door.

2. THE TWO BEARS

The two Bears were my co-workers and closest friends in New Oraibi. They lived in a tiny two-room apartment in a gaunt old house down the road. I took my meals with them and bathed and shaved in their bathroom.

White Bear collected most of our research material. He would take down on a little battery-run tape recorder the discourses of our Hopi spokesmen. Later he would play them back, translating them into English to his wife who would type them for my use. He also served as my interpreter when I interviewed Hopis, guided me to all the mentioned sites of ancient ruins and hidden shrines, and made drawings of pictographs and petroglyphs carved on rocks and cliffs.

He was fifty-three years old and looked twenty years younger. Like most Hopis, he was short and a little plump, with a dark full-moon face that usually wore a placid expression. Wearing his favorite porkpie hat, he looked like a lovable kewpie.

Oswald Fredericks was his legal name and the name by which he was better known to almost all Hopis. The "Government," according to its early custom, had given the English name of Fredericks to his family. It was a large family comprising six brothers, one of whom was his father; and another his uncle, Wilson Fredericks, better known as the controversial Village Chief of Old Oraibi, Tawakwaptiwa. Why White Bear, Kocha Honowah, had been given this Bear Clan name puzzled me, for according to custom he belonged to his mother's Coyote Clan. But he was inordinately proud, with good reason, of his relationship to his father's Bear Clan. For Old Oraibi, now crumbling into ruins, had been regarded as the parental home of Hopi ceremonialism; and a member of the Bear Clan was always chosen as its Village Chief, making him the virtual religious leader of the Hopis.

White Bear as a child, like all Hopi children, had been initiated into one of the two societies to which all Hopis belonged. This ordinarily was followed, when the boy grew into a youth, by induction into one of the major religious societies which conducted the great ceremonies in the annual cycle. White Bear, instead, was sent to the Indian School in Phoenix, and thereafter to Haskell Institute in Lawrence, Kansas, and Bacon College in Muskogee, Oklahoma. Here he became a devout Christian and went East to work many years for the Boy Scouts in New York City, the Y.M.C.A. in Newark, and for Fred Waring at Shawnee-on-the-Delaware.

Returning to Arizona, he met his future wife on a golf course in Phoenix. She was a blue-eyed, straw-haired white woman of German descent, short and plump, and extroverted by nature. Born in Waukegan, Illinois, she had been previously married and divorced, and had led a successful business life in Chicago. Her given name was Naomi, but she liked to call herself Brown Bear, because, as she said, "My skin is white but my heart is Hopi."

A few years after their marriage the two Bears returned to White Bear's home Reservation. There was no hotel, motel, boarding house, or restaurant in New Oraibi save a large, rambling house owned by White Bear's aunt who occasionally took in visitors—the same building containing the small apartment in which they were now living. This Brown Bear took over and ran with great dispatch. She was an excellent cook and efficient manager, and knew how to handle people. I met them that summer when I was camping at a spring nearby. White Bear was ill and generally kept out of the way. Yet the few times I talked with him, I became aware of the conflicting aspects of his character.

His many years away had given him a devout belief in Christianity and a modern white perspective on life, a white wife, and a love of golf. At the same time, paradoxically, these years had nur-

15

tured an equally strong belief in the religious traditions of his people. It took shape, as he lay alone and lonely in boarding houses and hall bedrooms, in the idealistic vision of a Hopi Camelot standing on its clifftop, resplendent, pure, and untouched by mortal frailty. So it had stood in the past and would stand again. Like a messiah, he prophesied a rejuvenation of ancient Hopi belief and the restoration of crumbling Oraibi as a citadel of Bear Clan domination once his people had thrown off the yoke of white oppression.

Brown Bear's venture was not successful. When the few summer visitors petered out, the two Bears returned discouraged to Phoenix, where White Bear obtained a job as instructor in arts and crafts at the Boys Club. Their great break came shortly thereafter when they happened to meet, on his trip West, the director of the "Angel of Wall Street's" Foundation, which was sponsoring a project to aid the Apaches. White Bear convinced him of the value of helping to restore the Hopis' confidence in the future by exhuming their past. So the Angel initiated the project and secured a writer recommended by White Bear. The venture was not successful and the writer soon abandoned the work. Months later White Bear suggested me.

My first appraisal of the projected study was not reassuring. White Bear played me a tape recording of his version of the Creation myth, relating how the Creator had shaped clay in the semblance of a man and placed it in an oven to bake. Unfortunately it was left in too long and came out black. The Creator tried again. This time the clay figure came out too pale, a white man. The third time the Creator took no chances. He opened the oven door and poked his finger in the clay to see if it were cooked enough. It was just right; the clay figure was alive and colored a lovely red-brown, like Indians; but of course it had a hole in its belly as we all have had ever since.

This Belly Button Story, as it was termed by our Indians at Taos who invariably told it to inquisitive tourists, made me a little suspicious of White Bear. His obsessive desire to record his people's valid religious beliefs could not be doubted. But it was obvious that he did not know the essential detail and dignity, the scope and depth of the material that would be required. It also raised the one overriding question: whether the Hopis, obdurately secretive as I knew them to be, would talk freely. A few weeks later in New York, at a meeting with the Angel of Wall Street, White Bear assured us that the Hopis were devoutly eager to record their traditions and beliefs for posterity. He submitted the names of many influential Hopi elders whom he said had assented to serve as our spokesmen. Accordingly the Foundation approved a second attempt on the study and I agreed to direct it.

So the two Bears moved back to New Oraibi to begin work. A month later they wrote me in Taos, New Mexico; they were ready for me to come. They had secured for me the small two-room apartment in the big house of White Bear's aunt. They themselves would live in a house on the hill below Pumpkin Seed Point belonging to White Bear's mother. Accordingly I packed up my belongings and drove to New Oraibi to live for the winter.

When I arrived I found the Bears installed in the small apartment presumably rented for me; they had decided I was to live in the house at Pumpkin Seed Point. This, however, was in such a dilapidated state that it was uninhabitable and I found myself without a place to live.

Since my own house was now closed up for the winter, I had no choice but to drive to Los Angeles to do some museum research until the Bears had fixed up the house. "Don't write me to come this time until the house is ready for me to move into," I warned them.

A month later White Bear telephoned, assuring me the house was now completely ready. "Meet us at Moencopi on Sunday at noon. There's a dance going on," he said. "And bring some fresh hamburger," added Brown Bear. "It will save us driving to Flagstaff."

The request puzzled me, but I arrived at Moencopi Sunday noon with a case of coffee, a big turkey, and fixings for Thanksgiving—and fresh hamburger. Moencopi was an outlying Hopi village not quite midway between Flagstaff and New Oraibi. A Basket Dance was in progress and the village was swarming with Hopis and Navajos. But no Bears. At sundown I left for New Oraibi, wondering what had happened to them. On the way out of the village I met them driving in. They had driven to Flagstaff for a day's outing. I followed them back to New Oraibi, only to find that the house had not been prepared for me. It was necessary to spend three days helping White Bear carry old furniture from his aunt's house. As there was no water and no cook stove, Brown Bear decided I was to take all my meals with them. Her intensely practical nature now aggressively asserted itself. There was no other place within thirty miles to buy a meal or cup of coffee. Therefore I was to pay her city restaurant prices for meals, plus a city rental rate for the house. As we might be forced to live on Navajo mutton and canned goods bought at the trading post much of the time, these charges were ridiculously exorbitant. After several days of argument, Brown Bear surlily agreed to accept a monthly board and lodging rate large enough, I thought, to cover also their own expenses for food and rent.

It also seemed strange to me that after two months' residence in New Oraibi, White Bear had not yet done any work on the project. The reason was reflected by a change in his attitude that threw the two conflicting aspects of his character into sharp focus.

Out in the white world, he was cheerfully, aggressively White Bear of the Bear Clan, Old Oraibi, a spokesman for all his people. Here in New Oraibi and throughout the Reservation he was demurely Oswald Fredericks, abnormally shy and retiring. He had lost completely his self-confidence and proud assertiveness. He was timidly hesitant to meet other Hopis who participated in the sacred kiva rites to which he was not admitted, and could hardly be induced to call upon the influential elders whose cooperation he had promised us. If he did happen to meet one of them, he was reluctant to ask him to record his discussion on tape.

"The people don't want to talk," he said surlily. "They're suspicious of you."

"They haven't seen me yet," I reminded him quietly.

"You've got to project yourself like a Hopi!" shouted Brown Bear angrily. "Like I do! My skin is white but my heart is Hopi!"

Indians are Indians. Information about their religious beliefs and practices is spiritual property. It is not to be given away lightly. Moreover, these Hopis have been always the most secretive and obdurate of all tribes, the reason why they have been so enigmatic to professional ethnologists. Even White Bear, when he did begin to obtain some specific information, was reluctant to part with it. So from deep within him, where they had been submerged for so many years under a veneer of conscious Christian-white values, there began to well up all the unconscious attributes of the traditional Hopi.

The emergence of this psychological conflict in my co-worker, difficult as it made things for us, revealed to me a tribal aspect of the Hopis I had not glimpsed before. I remembered an accomplished ethnologist who had established residence here to study the Hopis, but had finally given up the effort because she could never feel at home among them as she had with other Indian groups.

Beneath their kind and placid demeanor, the characteristic usually commented upon by most casual observers, I began to detect in all their talks an embittered condemnation of the white world's dominating injustices, alternating with unqualified assertions that Hopi ritualism contained the exclusive secret of universal life. Natural as this was, it made me feel distinctly uneasy. It is so easy for us, as well as the Hopis, to blame all our misfortunes and defects on others; to nurse in secret the superior sanction which makes us different from the rest of mankind. Yet it is exactly this which fatally exiles an individual, or a nation, from others, depriving him of the healing communion with the whole society of man. It is the sign of a messianic compulsion of an individual, or a race, possessed by the mythology of an inherent superiority. What this mythological content of the Hopis was, I did not yet know; I had received but a few pages of translated talks.

"I don't have time to type if I have to cook three times a day!" angrily shouted Brown Bear. "Why don't you do it yourself!"

I felt sorry for her. Now for the first time she was stuck in an alien world, knowing not one word of Hopi and nothing of Hopi custom and tradition, and without a white person to visit. Three times a day she had to cook for the three of us. The rest of the day she was obliged to sit at the typewriter, taking down White Bear's translation of the recorded tapes. There were no amusements for an extroverted woman accustomed to city life. No relief from a perpetual grind. So there began within her, as within White Bear, and between them both, the unconscious conflict between the Indian and the white.

"I'm getting tired of Navajo mutton and canned goods," she would say every few days. "Let's drive to Flagstaff and lay in a supply of good meat and fresh vegetables. We'll stay overnight in a motel and see a movie!"

Or if something came up that looked as if I might be called away for a few days, she would suffer a toothache that needed attention in Sedona; or complain of arthritis, gall bladder trouble, sinus, or backache that would require a trip to Phoenix. "We'd better have a look at our house down there too," she would tell White Bear darkly. "We've got personal and business affairs too that need attention, and don't forget it!"

Anything to get AWAY, anywhere, on any excuse.

Our only relief was Mama Bear: White Bear's mother, Anna Fredericks, whose Hopi name was Tuvemyumse, Land Beautiful With Flowers. The tie between mother and child is very strong among Hopis. Marriage never breaks it, and White Bear always regarded her home as his own. It was a crude little house not far away, and Mama Bear came often to visit. She was all Hopi and completely integrated; a little woman with quick eyes, a tiny musical voice, and a sunny disposition.

I loved to listen to her stories during the storytelling period in December. Hopis are superb storytellers. An ordinary tale would take at least an hour to relate. It was usually about evil witches or benign spirits who plagued or assisted a human being in trouble. The art consisted of blending the natural and supernatural in a context of sensory impressions. No detail was omitted: the sheen of moonlight through the trees, the shape of a stone on which one stumbled, the feel of the wind through the hair, the sound of birds and animals talking—not only the sound but their detailed conversation.

Mama Bear was a master artist. She would start to tell her story straight, then lapse into minutes of rapid dialogue between several characters, and suddenly break into a tinkling little song. Leaning forward in her stiff-backed chair, her quick eyes would dart about the room and her little feet would play out from her

21

skirts like little birds. Her English was adequate, but she would soon switch to Hopi with frequent pauses in order to let White Bear translate as he sat carving a kachina doll out of a chunk of cottonwood. When she had finished her nightly tale, Brown Bear would wrap up some cookies or a piece of cake for her, and White Bear would carefully escort her home by flashlight. Then I too would walk slowly home to the little house below Pumpkin Seed Point.

My way led past a small room dug into the side of the hill just below my house. As I trudged by, I would see the light of a lamp faintly glowing behind the blanket hung over the tiny window. Here Papa Bear, White Bear's father, a lonely recluse, spent most of his time. Charles Fredericks, or Tuwahoyiwma, Land Animals, must have been a sensitive and intelligent man when young. He had been selected to replace his uncle as Village Chief of Old Oraibi when Chief Lololma died a half-century or more ago. He refused, saying that he did not yet have full knowledge of the great Bear Clan ceremony, Soyal. Perhaps he had other reservations about living in strife-torn Oraibi and filling so difficult a post. So Tawakwapitwa, one of his five brothers, was named chief. Papa Bear then moved down into New Oraibi, adopted Christianity, and for a time carried mail for the agency at Keams Canyon.

Now, almost sixty years later, I would occasionally see him walking home with a slow, measured stride. A tragic figure, tall, slim, and bent, with a lean, tortured face. But most of the time he remained shut up in his little dark room in the hillside. Reading *The New Testament* by the dim light of the tiny window. Then carving out kachinas of his first faith, the great Soyal, meticulous in every detail. A man trying to bridge two worlds, belonging wholly to neither.

Chief Tawakwaptiwa was cast in a sterner mold, just as tragic. Soon after he had been named chief, the government decreed that he should be deprived of his chieftainship until he learned the English language and American customs. So he was packed off to Sherman Institute at Riverside, California. Four years later he came back thoroughly indoctrinated as a "Friendly," or one amenable to agency control, yet a chief upon whom it was incumbent to uphold the "Hostile" customs and religious traditions of his people. Tawakwaptiwa served neither master. He straddled the fence as a shrewd and irascible politician. Hopis and white alike reported him quarrelsome, treacherous, and vindictive.

It was his lot to rule over a decaying capital and dying culture. Half of his people moved out to found the new village of Hotevilla. Other families moved down to the settlement of New Oraibi being built up by Americanized and Christianized Hopis. One by one the great ceremonies were abandoned.

So now he sat up in the crumbling ruins of Old Oraibi, an aging and wasting old man with straggly gray hair, complacently regarding the disintegration around him as a confirmation of Prophecy—eking out an existence by carving kachina dolls, making lightning sticks, and decorating gourd rattles to sell to stray tourists. His kachina dolls were all strangely shaped like sausages, without limbs and semblance of life. They reminded me of zeppelins ready for flight. Like them, the old chief was ready to go.

Everyone talked about his impending death and conjectured who would succeed him. Papa Bear was in line, but he was too old and would certainly refuse again. Would White Bear be named? We ourselves wondered.

"Why not?" I asked him. "Certainly no man is being prepared as thoroughly as you are by the work you're doing now. What other Hopi will know so much about his people's beliefs and history—the creation of all the worlds, the routes of all the clans' migrations, the meanings of all the ceremonies, their complete history. . . . If you'll only get it!"

"It was prophesied when I was a boy that I would be the eyes, ears, and voice of my people," White Bear said slowly.

"Of course he won't get all that material!" broke out Brown Bear. "He's a procrastinator! He's never done a thing on time all the years we've been married. He procrastinates! Besides, he's not like these ignorant, illiterate Hopis. He's been out in the white world long enough to know what really matters nowadays!"

White Bear did not reply. He sat there before us, his gentle hands folded in his lap, staring with his kind and luminous brown eyes at that idealistic vision growing clearer and sharper every day. At an evil world destroyed by cataclysm save for the Hopis who would reestablish the plan of the Creator under the guidance of a new leader above all reproach.

Bad weather set in. We all suffered cabin fever from our enforced intimacy. Work proceeded so slowly that I grew impatient and irascible, and when I was away I fancied that I could hear the two Bears grumbling against that Dodagee, the Dictator. "You're kind enough to animals and children," Brown Bear accused me forthrightly, "but you're sure hell on grown-ups!"

Our project had got off to a bad start and we all doubted that it would ever be finished. I often wondered if at best it would be any more than an indictment of a modern civilization that had suppressed the outmoded culture of its conquered native people without giving them its own. But how could this be? For no ancient culture can be entirely repressed; its archaic gods and demons eventually spring forth as disastrously as Wotan erupted from the minds of Hitler's Germany. Races and nations are made up of individuals and their conflicts must be resolved on this deeper level of understanding. It was quite evident that our own work, contrary to that of professional anthropologists, was more than compiling facts; it had to proceed from the inside out, keeping pace with Hopi thought.

3. THE DREAMS

Among the events that helped to break the ice for us that first winter was a series of strange dreams that came to me. They began in a curious manner soon after the mysterious incident of gravel being thrown against the window pane.

Entering the two Bears' apartment late one afternoon, I saw an old man in his late seventies sitting on the couch with White Bear. He was dressed in a ragged red sweater and baggy pants, his straggly gray hair falling in bangs to his chin and tied with homespun cotton into a chignon in back. Tears were streaming down his dark, wrinkled face. He would wipe them off with a hand still darker and more wrinkled, and continue talking into the tape recorder. He gave the impression of a man torn by a wracking sincerity. His words, interpreted by White Bear, bore this out.

"I don't blame the white people for their genius to transmit power through their many kinds of machines. But I am not impressed with these machines. They are crude mechanical contraptions that may break down. We Hopis don't need them. We know how to manifest our powers—the same powers—without machines. I will tell you about these powers and how the stars help us. It won't do any good. For our First World was destroyed because the people became evil, then the Second World, and the Third World. Now we are on the Fourth World and we have become evil too and it will be destroyed. But let me tell you. Without my people, without any people left in the world at all, I will still conduct my ceremony, singing and praying to the sun to project his power by silent vibrations so that we may continue our life on the next, Fifth World. Thus I will fulfill my ordained duty."

He stayed for dinner and gratefully accepted a package of cigarettes before White Bear drove him home. White Bear returned elated. Don Qochhongva, he said, was the chief religious leader in Hotevilla. He was going to tell us all he knew. Moreover he was going to persuade all the other religious, kiva, and clan chiefs to help us too. Our worries were over!

"I told him about that gravel. He trusts you. He said to tell you that you will now have four important dreams. You will see!"

A couple of nights later the first one came.

I was suddenly aware that there were two men in the room. My first impulse was to jump out of bed and throw the catch on the door as I had been told. But the men were already inside and looked quite harmless. They were probably two traveling salesmen, old-fashioned drummers of the sort who occasionally drove through the Reservation peddling knickknacks from house to house. One was dressed in a reddish-brown suit with one coat button off, and the other in a rumpled dark blue suit.

"Don't be alarmed," said the man in the reddish-brown suit. "We're ghosts, and you should know that ghosts are just like people except that they live in a world invisible to you. We travel in great migrations, something like wild geese, along a traditional route from way above Bering Strait down to the tip of South America. My own home base between trips is northern Alaska. My partner here hails from the lower Argentine."

The one in the dark blue suit was just as sensible and friendly although his voice sounded a little more stern.

"We've dropped by to tell you that this place is directly on our route back and forth between the poles. You're on the line now. Mind what I say. Stay on the line now."

Next morning I related this occurrence to White Bear at breakfast. He was curiously excited and demanded full details.

"No, I don't remember their faces at all," I explained. "Just their clothes. I couldn't tell their race or nationality. So it must have been a dream. Anyway the light was out when I awoke this morning."

White Bear rushed over to Mama Bear's house and then drove up to see old Don Qochhongva. When he came back, he assured me that my visitors had been the sacred Twins, Palongawhoya and Poqanghoya, one of whom was stationed at the north pole of the world axis and the other at the south pole. Their duties were to keep the earth properly rotating and to send out calls for good or warning through the vibratory centers of the earth.

"See? You're on the line to receive their vibratory messages," White Bear told me. "You must be careful to stay on the line as they told you."

The second dream came within a week.

I dreamed that I was driving my car back from Hotevilla on the high northwestern tip of the mesa. The downhill grade was very steep, swinging around the bend of the cliff walls. This semi-circle of sheer rock escarpments enclosed a high valley sloping down to the flat desert below. It was barren and forbidding, littered with huge boulders and debris from the talus slopes of the cliffs. But suddenly it filled with a glowing pink light beautiful beyond description. As I swung closer round the bend I saw that the valley was completely filled with a thick orchard of cherry, peach, and apricot trees whose branches and blossoms filtered the sunlight with the strange pinkish glow. At the same moment, I could feel the warmth of the glow suffusing my whole body.

When I told the two Bears about the dream next morning, Brown Bear exclaimed at once, "Isn't that the place, Bear, where you said some geologists found oil but couldn't get permission to dig? Oil wells are going to sprout there, all right. It's Bear Clan land too, isn't it? You better see that your claim to it is established right away!"

"A good dream!" said White Bear, his face beaming like a full Hopi moon. "That's the place where the racetrack and stone piles of the Twins are, the shrines of the Oaqol and Lalakon maidens, and all the rock writing. Everything is going to blossom out for us. We will ask Old Dan!"

Old Dan Qochhongva, I had found out, was generally considered the foremost religious leader not only of Hotevilla but virtually of all other Hopi villages. This mantle of leadership had been won with difficulty. Back in the 1880's, Chief Lololma of Oraibi had been taken to Washington where he was persuaded to cooperate with the government. Opposition developed under the leadership of Yukioma, Old Dan's father, who accused Lololma and his followers of being too friendly to the government and too progressive. Yukioma and his followers insisted that all Hopis, like themselves, adhere to their own traditional way of life. As evidence of their faith, they refused to send their children to school. Thus there developed two factions: the Friendlies under Chief Lololma and the Hostiles or Traditionals under Yukioma.

Trouble developed when a troop of Negro cavalry arrived to enforce Americanization of all Hopis. Lololma, shamed and betrayed, died of a broken heart. Tawakwaptiwa assumed leadership and continued the quarrel with Yukioma. It came to a head in the famous Oraibi Split when the two factions, in order to avoid bloodshed, agreed to a tug of war to decide the issue. Yukioma and his Traditionals lost. That night they left Oraibi forever—nearly 300 men, women, and children—and camped on the site of what soon became the new village of Hotevilla.

During the fierce but bloodless battle, Old Dan, then a young man, was struck on the head and lay unconscious and unheeded, for his father had decreed that if anyone were struck down he was not to be touched. Finally he regained consciousness, swearing an oath that he would always uphold his people's traditions. This religious enlightenment stood him in good stead.

More cavalry troops arrived to dig naked and frightened children out of their hiding places and to cart them off to school. Yukioma resisted and was carried off to the Keams Canyon agency where he was jailed for seventeen years. Despite the imprisonment of this "American Dalai Lama," as the agent called him, the contentious village of Hotevilla prospered under his son's obdurate traditionalism. As fast as the ceremonies were given up at dying Oraibi, they were adopted at Hotevilla. By 1929 Oraibi's eight centuries of rule were over. Hotevilla had become the center of Hopi ceremonialism. Yukioma had died and Old Dan had assumed leadership. Now approaching eighty, he still held the reins in his aging, wrinkled hands.

There was something deeply significant about this historic Oraibi Split, as I found out, for it brought to surface for the first time the inner schism that had been developing since the arrival of the first white men. I began to sense in Old Dan an unusual man for trusting to the guidance of his inner promptings against forceful outside opposition, as a result of his religious enlightenment while he was unconscious. I was eager to hear what he might say about my second dream.

It was not yet eight o'clock in the evening when White Bear and I drove up to see him, but Hotevilla was already dark and lifeless. How eerie it was to grope through the narrow, sand-drifted, and refuse-littered streets behind the beam of a flashlight! The gloom was not dispelled when we found and entered his house. Five or six persons were squatting on the floor, shelling corn on a blanket. The process looked simple, as they merely scraped the kernels off with an empty cob. The trick was to keep the kernels from flying all over the room. It might have been a homey, jolly scene, but in the dim light of a smoking kerosene lamp that no one turned down it took on a somber aspect. No one laughed or talked or sang. When Old Dan came in all stopped working, the women crouching in the corner, the men sitting quietly with bowed heads.

Old Dan dominated the room with an hour of steady talk. Head thrown back, eyes half-closed, hands clutching his ragged red sweater, he never stopped for breath. I began nudging White Bear to translate. He ignored me.

I was reminded of the story of an attaché who accompanied an American woman visiting in Germany to hear, in the Reichstag, a speech by the Chancellor, a famous orator. Minute after minute went by without a word of translation from the attaché. In desperation the lady finally poked him in the ribs and whispered, "What is he saying?" The attaché flung her a look of annoyance. "Madame! I am waiting for the verb!"

Like the lady, I finally gave White Bear a stiff poke and demanded, "What does he say?"

"He said your dream was good and the third one will come soon. He has all the leaders lined up to help us."

As we drove home an hour later, White Bear added another bit of information. Old Dan was going to enter the kiva next day to begin the purification rites for the coming ceremony. "If my heart is right during my duties tomorrow," he had said, "the clouds will gather above me." His name, Qochhongva, meant in English "White Clouds Above Horizon." The next evening for the first time in many days the clouds were piling up in a rosy flare at sunset.

It was now late in November and the first of the great ceremonies in the annual cycle was beginning. Wúwuchim was a solemn and important ceremony. It recreated the first dawn of Creation and was a ceremonial supplication for the germination of all forms of life on earth—plant, animal, and man. No white man, and no Hopis save its participating members, were allowed to witness its major ritual. It was so sacred and so secret that people referred to it only as Astotokya, the Night of the Washing of the Hair—a night of terror and mystery. Old Dan conducted the ceremony as the chief of the Two Horn society. Its symbol of two great curved horns which the priests wore on their heads designated their knowledge of the three previous worlds as well as this present Fourth World. Old Dan was now immured in the kiva to conduct sixteen days and nights of secret rituals before the public ceremony on the last day. We were fortunate indeed to have the promise of his support, and I looked forward to the third dream or vision he had foretold for me.

It came while he was still in the kiva and took the shape of a vivid fantasy.

I was awakened one night by the sound of someone walking around the house. A measured, steady tread, accompanied by a curious, faint rattle at every step. As I listened, the pace of the steps increased, the rattling grew louder, until it seemed as though the house were encircled by running figures. I flung out of bed and rushed to the window. No one, nothing moving, was visible in the moonlight. The sound increased in pace and volume, rising in pitch to a steady whine. The feeling suddenly struck me that I was encircled by a swiftly revolving ring at once invisible and impenetrable. What it might be I could not imagine. I dared not open the door and stick my head outside; I felt curiously safe within the house. I went back to bed. A moment later, with a last shrill and hollow whine, the sound suddenly stopped and I fell asleep.

Old Dan interpreted it later when he taped an explanation of the entire Wúwuchim ceremony. At the beginning of the ceremony a line of cornmeal was drawn on the ground around the kiva to seal it off from all trespassers. On the dread Night of the Washing of the Hair all roads were also closed by cornmeal, and villagers living in houses close to the kiva were evacuated. To further protect the initiates from all worldly contamination, Two Horn and One Horn guards kept encircling the kiva. Each carried a long lance and wore on his left leg a turtle shell rattle which sounded the stamp of his measured tread. As the crucial hour approached when the initiates went through a re-enactment of the Emergence, other-world spirits then came to encircle the kiva with whirling rings of invisible power.

If there were any doubts as to the astounding similarity between this ritual and my own fantasy, they were dispelled on the last day of the ceremony when I saw the Two Horn and One Horn priests come out of the kiva, stamping their rattle legs as they successively encircled the kiva, the plaza, the village, and surrounding shrines. A weird and barbarically beautiful procession of fantasmal shapes gliding from dusk into the darkness of an immeasurable past.

My fourth dream followed in ceremonial sequence as preparations were being made for Soyal, the second ceremony, whose major rite was timed to coincide with the winter solstice. Soyal was one of the greatest of all Hopi ceremonies. It symbolized the second phase of Creation at the dawn of life, when all the life germinated during Wúwuchim made its first appearance in living forms and man was initiated into the mystery of his being.

I knew nothing about the rites as yet, but I dreamed that I was sitting in a kiva on a low bench in the middle of the floor. The light was dim, but I could see that the bench was placed on a cornmeal line that ran from east to west as if marking the path of the sun's journey overhead. An altar loomed before me.

I paid no attention to it, for someone was behind me. All I could see were the hands that reached around me to unfasten the belt at my waist. They were old and dark and wrinkled. They took off all my clothes—every stitch. Then they washed my hair in soapy water. I could tell by the smell that the suds were made by *amole,* the roots of soap-weed yucca. When this was done, a tiny hawk feather was tied to the hair at the top of my head and over my shoulders was thrown a beautiful cape—pure white, hand-woven, a little coarse but soft as cotton.

All this time I was sitting with my bare legs stretched out before me and with my hands in my lap. Those strange dark hands now lifted my feet to the bench, and placed my own hands under my armpits so that my elbows stuck out on each side. It was an uncomfortable position.

In a little while the hands reappeared with a bowl of queer-tasting liquid which I was given to drink. I didn't like its faint odor either; it took me some time to drink it down. After this I was left alone, still sitting in that awkward, winglike position.

My arms and legs began to cramp. Then I began to feel ill from the bowl of liquid I had drunk. It made me want to vomit and to go to the toilet. This I seemed to know was impossible; there just wasn't anywhere to go. So I sat there, gagging, cramped, and uncomfortable. Waiting for what? A taxi to arrive and drive me off in a hurry! A New York taxi with a little yellow light on top and a meter clicking away inside! It didn't come, and the next thing I knew I was awake in bed feeling quite comfortable. . . .

Old Dan seemed pleased by the dream, but made only one direct comment. The liquid given me to drink was *ngakuyi,* a medicine-water made from bones of fierce animals such as the bear, mountain lion, and wolf, ground and mixed with water. It was drunk for inner purification, reacting on the nervous centers of the body. Ordinarily it did not make anyone sick, he said, but to one of a different race like myself it might possibly act as an emetic.

As Soyal was predominantly a Bear Clan ceremony, we also went to Papa Bear for an explanation of its rituals. He confirmed the use of *ngakuyi* by all participating members and described how a path of cornmeal was drawn from east to west, symbolizing the Road of Life for all plants, birds, animals, and men on earth. All these forms of life were symbolically hatched by a woman who was escorted into the kiva and seated on a specially woven plaque filled with seeds and prayer feathers. Here she squatted like a setting hen during the ceremony, patiently hatching the germinated seeds and prayers of her people. She was commonly called Hawk Maiden because the young neophytes or initiates were always called *kekelt,* fledgling hawks. Naked save for a white cotton *manta* thrown over their shoulders, and a tiny hawk feather tied to the hair at the top of their heads, they were made to sit with their feet up, hands tucked under their armpits and elbows sticking out. This signified that they were fledglings too weak yet to fly with their spiritual wings. How often I saw them later in the kivas! Little boys patiently squatting in their cramped positions, watching with mesmeric wonder the strange masked shapes dancing before them.

This series of dreams that had come as foretold by Old Dan had a cumulative effect upon me. Not only were they dreams about an esoteric religion I was yet unfamiliar with, but they had portrayed aspects of its rituals in advance of the ceremonies themselves. How progressively they had built up! The first dream of two ghosts had told me that I was "on the line" to receive knowledge. This had been followed by a glowing promise of fruition. I had then been symbolically immured in a kiva, and later I had been given my first initiation as a fledgling hawk. All four were so literal that they left me only one interpretation. Old Dan, in some manner, had led me to a dream-initiation into the mysteries of the ceremonies upon which we were then working. I felt a strange and warm attachment to this obdurate old mystic in his ragged red sweater, and looked forward to more dreams under his guidance.

They never came. For suddenly the coin of his nature, like that of most Hopis, flipped over to reveal its obverse side.

Things had been building up step by step to the climax. White Bear kept relying on Old Dan's promise to obtain prominent spokesmen for us. Old Dan kept putting him off. Finally he agreed to call a meeting of kiva and clan leaders at which we would explain to them the purpose of our study and ask their cooperation.

One night they all came down from Hotevilla—Old Dan and a half-dozen of his leaders. For three hours they sat talking, listening, talking some more. Finally they left, saying they would think it over and let us know.

A week later Old Dan sent word that one of his leaders had turned against us, saying we were being paid by the government to ferret out Hopi secrets to use against them. The meeting, explained Old Dan, had been merely a ruse by which he could find out which one of his leaders was disloyal to him. Now he knew and would drop him.

His rival we knew as "Mister Hopi." Feared and mistrusted by many Traditionals throughout the Reservation, he had two traits distinctly non-Hopi: an aggressive lust for power and an itch for publicity. Openly declaring himself a staunch Traditional, he yet curried favor with the younger faction of Americanized Hopis and members of the government-sponsored Tribal Council which rubber-stamped the decisions of the agency on all secular matters. He dressed well, spoke excellent English, and was constantly writing letters datelined the "Hopi Empire." At the same time he was not above letting out tidbits of religious tradition to visiting ethnologists, government officials, and prominent tourists who would quote him as a spokesman.

Finally the matter came to a head. White Bear and I were called to another meeting in Mister Hopi's own home. Here he blatantly informed us that it had been determined we were either government or church spies, and that none of the leaders would be permitted to give us any information. Old Dan did not utter a word in our defense during the long harangue. He sat, head tilted back, eyes half closed, his thin wasting body visibly shrinking before our eyes. Feeling too ashamed of him to be sorry for him, we left without a word.

His betrayal of us shook White Bear badly. After a sleepless night, he came to me pale and defeated. "It's all over! We can't go on. We must drop the project! It has been prophesied."

"Not on your life!" I shouted back just like Dodagee, the Dictator. "We're not going to be stopped by that cowardly old reprobate or Mister Hopi either! We're going out and find other spokesmen, loyal Hopis who are sincere in what they believe!"

A great deal more lay behind this incident than was apparent —the whole complex web of Hopi traditionalism. The Bear Clan was the leading clan, but there were no Bear Clan members in Hotevilla, for its dissenting founders, when leaving Oraibi, had been largely members of Yukioma's Fire or Ghost Clan. Since by tradition leadership should pass from the Bear Clan to the Parrot Clan and then the Tobacco Clan, many Hopis refused to accept the leadership of the Fire Clan. If this tradition of clan succession seemed complex, another factor beclouded matters still more.

Old Dan, being Yukioma's son, was not of the Fire Clan; according to custom he belonged to his mother's Sun Clan. Hence

Yukioma's rightful successor was the son of his sister, a man known as James, who belonged to the Fire Clan. James, however, had been away for some time and in trouble. So Old Dan had assumed leadership during his absence. Now that he was getting old and his power was waning, Mister Hopi emerged as a would-be contender for leadership. Mister Hopi, however, belonged to a minor clan without a ceremony or any standing whatever. He needed something with which he could nudge tottering Old Dan off his insecure throne. That, I saw now, was Old Dan's disgraceful sponsorship of us two spies under the bountiful pay of the government or a white church. It had worked. We were out, and it looked as if Old Dan were out too. Still, one never knew. Old Dan was not the son of the indomitable and irascible Yukioma for nothing. In the intricate game of Hopi politics he might merely have sacrificed White Bear and me to gain more worthy ends. The incident, tragic-comic as it was, turned out to our advantage. But I missed Old Dan.

It was months before I saw him again. A public meeting was called in the abandoned schoolhouse near Shongopovi on Second Mesa. Mister Hopi and his cohorts were there in a vociferous body to protest the acceptance of state welfare benefits by any impoverished Hopis because such dependence would destroy their faith in the Creator. After the meeting was over, I happened to see Old Dan come limping up the road in his ragged red sweater. Mister Hopi and his other former leaders had not offered to bring him. So Old Dan had walked and hitchhiked the twenty miles. He did not speak, but I saw in his sweat-filled eyes a look of warm recognition and ironic amusement.

What an admirable old rascal he was! Dispossessed in the field of secular affairs, like Yukioma, he functioned only in the mystic realm of rituals, dreams, and visions—a true Hopi.

I thought a great deal about dreams that winter. Most dreams seemed to me no more than unconscious reflections of the day's surface happenings of which we had been aware; one could attach little significance to them. Such an attitude was typical of the average white. To almost all Hopis, on the contrary, constant dreams, visions, and fantasies were a commonly accepted part of their daily lives. They depended upon them for personal guidance and to foretell future events for their people. These "voices of prophecy" were ancient gods, archetypal symbols and images speaking from the lowest level of the unconscious. C. G. Jung termed this bottom level the impersonal or "collective unconscious" because it embodied the contents of the primeval past common to all humanity, distinguishing it from the upper level of the personal unconscious distinctive to each individual.

Reading the many studies of both Jung and Neumann, I began to understand the origin of these psychic dream components in the unconscious and the layers through which they rose to consciousness. I began to perceive the differences between casual top-level dreams and these dreams at depth. Rising into consciousness, their forms were of course molded by the psychology of the individual dreamer. But before they reached the perimeter of consciousness, something else, I was sure, helped to shape their forms. It seemed to me there must be a layer or level in the unconscious not postulated in any of the studies I had read: a layer interposed between the impersonal or collective unconscious and the personal unconscious. A filter that somehow embodied all the predispositions or inherited tendencies of the race to which the individual predominantly belonged.

Jung, who named the collective unconscious, was a Swiss-European. All his vast body of work reflected his own racial and cultural background, particularly the archetypes of ancient alchemy on which he was an authority. India's archetypal images and sym-

39

bols he strangely refused to accept, considering the universality he imputed to any archetype. "Shall we be able to put on, like a new suit of clothes, ready-made symbols grown on foreign soil, saturated with foreign blood, spoken in a foreign tongue, nourished by a foreign culture, interwoven with foreign history, and so resemble a beggar who wraps himself in kingly raiment, a king who disguises himself as a beggar?" he asked.

I, for one, on the contrary, have never had a dream in my life with a medieval European or alchemical background, although since childhood I have had dreams whose forms and backgrounds reflected the ancient pasts of both Asia and Africa. Nor have I ever known in my long acquaintance with them an American Indian or a Mexican Indian whose dream backgrounds were the Arthurian cycle and the quest of the Holy Grail, however universal is the meaning of their symbolism.

This difference seemed quite natural if one accepted, as I did, the fact that prenatal predispositions or inherent tendencies are embodied in each one of us on the basis of our own evolutionary past —that accumulated prehistory of causal effects termed karma by Eastern philosophers. We carry not only an individual karma, but a karma of the race and of the land mass to which we are attuned. All the past of all humanity lies stored in the collective unconscious of each of us. But in the rise of its archetypes into consciousness they are filtered through a racial layer which transforms them, *with unchanged meaning,* into familiar indigenous forms.

My dreams that lonely winter, then, posed a number of questions I could not answer. I was pleased to believe that I had soaked in enough Hopi ceremonialism for my four dreams to reflect it, aided by my own part-Indian heritage. But still I understood that these dreams referred not so much to the world of Hopi ceremonialism as to my own inner world. What were they trying to tell me?

Weeks later I had another strange dream. I was slowly climbing down a flight of stone stairs in the dark interior of what I felt was a pyramid. One flight terminated at a small level only to give way to another flight leading to one below. By the light of a candle I finally reached the bottom, a subterranean chamber closed off on all sides by solid dark walls.

Possessed by a growing uneasiness, I noticed imbedded in the floor a great bronze slab peculiarly shaped like a rectangular keyhole. Looked at more closely, it revealed the engraving of an ancient head, Egyptian or Mayan, wearing large earrings of the same shape as the slab itself. Around this was a border or frieze of similar, smaller heads. Suddenly a voice spoke. "Don't just stand there and look! Why don't you pull it up?"

I stooped, took hold of one of the large earrings, and pulled. It was the handle for the bronze slab which lifted easily as if it were on hinges, revealing an opening below. Just then I woke up.

White Bear, when I told him the dream, interpreted it literally, for the slab had the keyhole shape of many doorways found in prehistoric ruins throughout the Southwest and Mexico. For days thereafter he kept reminding me of other similar shapes we had not thought of before: the floor plan of many Hopi kivas; the visible portion of the kiva protruding above ground, the *kivaove,* "the part above"; the inlaid earrings worn by the Flute Maidens during the re-enactment of the Emergence to this Fourth World; and finally the outline of every Hopi man's head with his square-cut hair bangs falling down over his ears.

Uniquely Hopi as it seemed, the design was but a variation of the four-square, sacred symbol expressing a religious experience of wholeness common to all mankind. I myself, then, interpreted the dream as applying to me personally rather than exclusively to Hopi mythology. My lonely stay here among an alien people was leading me, as my dream showed, deeper and deeper into my own inner self. The very keyhole shape of the bronze slab indicated something that needed to be unlocked. What lay beneath it?

So every night after looking at the stars above Pumpkin Seed Point, I would settle in bed to view with greater wonder that vaster, unexplored realm within us—man's last, greatest, and most mysterious frontier.

4. THE PLAZA

The longer I stayed in New Oraibi the more restless and uninte-grated it seemed. I could not at first quite understand why; it is always the obvious that escapes notice.

The post office, isolated in a patch of sand, was always com-paratively deserted. One waited through the morning until the mail truck rumbled in from Winslow, then walked down for the day's mail, a necessary chore accomplished as quickly as possible. The lawn of the government school, so inviting on hot afternoons, was always just as deserted. Nor did people stand gossiping outside the church on Sunday mornings.

In one sense, the trading post seemed to be the focal point of town. A gasoline pump stood in front of it, and the town's only available telephone was mounted on a shelf on the outside wall. Here, freezing in winter cold or standing unprotected in pouring rain, one jiggled the hook for an hour before the operator in Hol-brook answered. There was no one to answer an incoming call. The trading post had been a famous one years ago when it was operated by the beloved Lorenzo Hubbell. Then it had been bought by a large mercantile company which operated it as one of many. During recent years it had been run by a succession of managers, none of whom had been liked by the Hopis. They claimed, for one thing, that the prices were far too high. For another, they insisted that the post showed preference to the many Navajos who drove in from the desert with turquoise and silver jewelry to pawn. What-ever the reasons for their dislike of the post, the Hopis, though obliged to trade in it, never lingered around it. Like the post office, school, and church, it was a utility building that served its purpose and nothing more.

As a government town, New Oraibi boasted a community hall. Standing just below Pumpkin Seed Point, it was a long, low cellar whose walls and roof protruded above ground just high enough to let light in through the windows. What it was used for I could not imagine until I was awakened one morning by the Village Crier announcing a public meeting there of the Tribal Council at nine o'clock.

Watching out the window of my house, I could see a few people beginning to arrive at ten o'clock. By eleven there was a sizable group standing outside. At noon I walked down to join some fifty people who were finally let inside. A hearty lunch had been prepared by women of the village, and when it was silently eaten the meeting began.

At a table up front sat the agent from Keams Canyon, a thin, sallow, sick man courageously enduring his tenure of government office until time for retirement; the tribal lawyer, an affluent Mormon from Utah; and the Tribal Council, comprised of representatives from all the villages except Hotevilla. The Tribal Council was sponsored by the government as a Hopi self-governing body entrusted with the management of all secular affairs. It and its supporters comprised the faction of Americanized Hopis known in Yukioma's time as the Friendlies. As such it was opposed by the Traditionalists who insisted on the right to govern their own affairs through the Village Chief. Hence the Traditional stronghold of Hotevilla refused to name a representative to the Tribal Council and to be bound by its decisions. It regarded the Council, as did many Hopis, as a concept of foreign white democracy, not representative of all the people, and without real authority as it was merely a puppet government controlled by the agency at Keams Canyon.

Talk got under way on several issues confronting all Hopis.

The Hopi Reservation comprised about 4,000 square miles located in the middle of the immense Navajo Reservation of nearly 25,000 square miles. The government had established it some eighty years ago with the solemn promise to protect it from Navajo encroachment. Yet now the swiftly growing tribe of 80,000 Navajos had so encroached on Hopi land that the 5,000 Hopis were confined to less than a fourth of their own Reservation. Hence a Hopi suit against the Navajo tribe was being drawn up. The outcome of the case would rest on proof that the Hopis owned and occupied the land prior to the coming of the Navajos. This occupancy could easily be proved, it was believed, by the existence of ancient ruins, rock writings, and secret shrines established long before the Navajos had migrated into the Southwest. Help was needed, for only the Hopi Traditionalists knew their locations and meanings.

The Traditionalists, however, stubbornly refused to impart the information. "Why hasn't the government kept the Navajos out as it promised. Why doesn't it now?" they asked.

Moreover, they opposed filing such a suit. The land had been given to the Hopis by their spiritual guardian long before the arrival of either the Navajos or the white man. They would never assent to having a white man's court decide whether their land belonged to them. As a matter of fact, they already had written to the Navajo Tribal Council saying that they would never authorize or recognize such a suit.

The subject was tabled for future discussion.

Another matter came up. An electric company had requested a franchise to build a line into the Reservation. Should the right-of-way be granted? There was a long, dreary silence. The Tribal Council members looked at each other's simple, puzzled faces in despair.

"Our land is not for leasing or for sale," a voice from the audience reminded them. "This is our sacred soil."

The agent rapped on the table with his gavel; the interjection was obviously out of order. The franchise was granted.

45

Approval was now requested of a new hospital being built by the Public Health Service at the Hopi agency headquarters, Keams Canyon, thirty miles east. The hospital had long been a contentious subject among Hopis. Why was it being built so far away from all Hopi villages? The answer was obvious: to accommodate encroaching Navajos who would admittedly fill ninety percent of its beds. Approval was duly voted.

The meeting dragged on, so boring that most of the few people in the audience got up and left. What could they do about the confused welter of secular affairs? They did not gather outside to discuss the issues, nor to gossip.

No, the community hall was not a community center. Nor was New Oraibi a Hopi village. It had no Village Chief; simply a governor elected by the Tribal Council. New Oraibi was merely a government town, a straggle of utility buildings without tradition, without meaning. There was no place to loaf, to gossip, to enjoy life. It had no center, no plaza. This, I finally realized, was what was wrong with New Oraibi.

Life on this continent from earliest times has revolved about a central plaza. The ruins of almost every prehistoric pueblo show it to have been a walled city or great terraced apartment house built around an inner court or plaza. Often rising five stories high and containing as many as 800 rooms, they were immense communal dwelling places, great fortresses breasting the solitude of earth and sky. There were few doors and windows. The entrance to each family's quarters was an opening cut in the roof. To reach it the people climbed up an outside ladder which they could pull up after them in case of attack by marauding tribes of nomads.

Defensively practical as the shapes of these great pueblos were, they also reflected the people's primary concern with the inner values of their lives. They were great mandalas. A mandala, the

46

Sanskrit word for circle, is a geometrical design expressive of the unity and wholeness of all Creation, a design which produces an effect upon its maker. Its basic form is that of a four-petalled lotus with infinite variations in the shape of a cross, a square, or a circle divided by four, but always with four as the basis of the structure. Mandalas have been found everywhere, in all ages. Christian mandalas show Christ in the center, with the four evangelists at the cardinal points, as in Egypt where Horus was represented in the same way with his four sons. Jung considered the mandalas of Tibetan Buddhism the most beautiful, and those found in the sandpaintings of the Pueblo Indians notable examples. The Hopi concept of a four-world universe, each world designated by a directional color, is itself a symbol of the soul-form of all Creation—a mandala. The superlative sandpaintings of the Navajos are undoubtedly the finest examples today. Made of natural colored sands sprinkled on the floor of a medicine hogan, they are an essential part of every healing ceremony. The patient is seated upon them, and at the conclusion of the songs, prayers, and rituals the medicine man sprinkles the sand upon him.

The ancient pueblos, whose terraced walls enclosed an inner court with circular or rectangular kivas in the center, were in effect great structural mandalas; and the subterranean kivas themselves— so diametrically opposite to the Christian church with its phallic spire—further symbolized the depths of the unconscious which held its meaning. The plaza, then, was the center of the people's outward communal life and the focus of their religious thought and ceremonies.

The contemporary Hopi villages—small, one-story, and tawdry as they were—deviated little from this ancient pattern. Each genuine Hopi village enclosed a quadrangular inner court or plaza, the *kisonvi* or "center of the village," dominated by one or more kivas.

The kiva, like the *kisonvi,* was rectangular in shape, both repeating the four-world universe, the four-square pattern of psychic wholeness. There was never any doubt as to the supreme significance of this mandala form. During the Niman Kachina ceremony when the kachinas emerged from the underground kiva into the open *kisonvi,* their dance was patterned and their song was built on its four-square shape, urging man to conform his life to this sacred pattern too.

The withdrawal of Old Dan's support had worked to our advantage. White Bear and I were forced out to all the villages where we found other spokesmen, all well informed, loyal, and eager to contribute to our effort. Winter and summer, day or night, we attended nearly every ceremony in every village, learning how every aspect of village life—family, communal, and religious—centered in the plaza.

We went often to Shongopovi. It was the largest village on Second Mesa and its ceremonies were the most colorful. The village had two plazas and looked out over the vast expanse of desert to the snow-capped mountains nearly a hundred miles southwest. Earl and Evelyn and their children always made us welcome. They lived in one large room opposite one of the kivas. The door was usually left open and we could see and hear everything that went on: the old men squatting against sunny walls, the constant parade of naked children, the circuits of kachinas, women shouting or gossiping from their own doorways, the braying of a burro. This was what New Oraibi lacked—life springing from a center.

Earl was a slightly built, neatly dressed man who was always tuning in a battery-run radio to cowboy songs. Evelyn, his wife, seemed his direct antithesis: a big, sturdy-framed woman with sharp black eyes and an unbounded capacity for work. Her hospitality lived up to Hopi tradition. A pot of coffee was always warming on the wood stove and usually a big pot of *knukwivi,* a stew of lamb and hominy, the customary meal. With this set on the table, we all gathered around, picking out chunks of meat with our fingers and spooning out hominy and juice with *piki,* the distinctive Hopi bread, made of finely ground cornmeal baked to a paper-thin cake on a piece of tin, then rolled up to the size of a large sausage. Crisp and delicately flavored, it came in all the colors of Hopi corn: white, yellow, red, and blue. Stacked like cordwood on a woven plaque, it made a wonderful sight. Evelyn always carried a huge plaque of it to the kiva when a ceremonial was under way, reserving another huge plaque for gifts to visitors. Preparation of it was an art and it required hours of work. She was no less adept at weaving plaques: stripping fiber from yucca leaves, staining it different colors, then coiling it into plaques that bore distinctive designs. Like a woman at a sewing bee, she seemed to do her best work when a group of neighbors came to sit on the floor and work with her.

The two smaller villages on Second Mesa, Mishongnovi and Shipaulovi, lay across the valley to the east on the end of another spur of Second Mesa. Both were spectacularly perched, like eagle eyries, on the tops of the two high, pyramidal buttes separated by a sloping hogback. One could drive past them in the valley below without distinguishing them from their rocky escarpments.

Shipaulovi was my favorite village. How tiny it was! Merely a cluster of rock houses surrounding a square plaza whose floor was solid rock. It gave an air of compactness, unity, and completeness that was reflected in the soft voices, gentle manners, and pleasant faces of its people. This feeling of confinement was artistically alleviated, as in the composition of a painting, by a passageway at the northwest corner. Like a Spanish *zaguan,* it was a deep and narrow hall roofed with cedar poles and brush that gave a view of the tremendous sweep of sky and desert. This was the entrance to the plaza used by dancers on the day of a ceremony. Standing here, you could see them winding up the rocky slope single file from the hidden shrine below like figures emerging from the earth.

Hotevilla on Third Mesa lay about ten miles north of New Oraibi. It could well have been built in the middle of the Sahara rather than on top of a mesa. Its main plaza was choked with drifting sand, and all around it stretched dunes of fine white sand out of which grew fields of corn and tiny peach orchards. Standing at the steep edge of the mesa, you could see more dunes rolling away in waves toward the desert beyond. Despite its dominant aridity, Hotevilla boasted several good springs. The village itself was named from a spring that gushed out of a cavern on the side of the cliff, so small that the roof scraped a man's back as he stooped to gather water. Hence the name of Hotevilla from *hote* (back) and *villa* (scratch). The water from another underground spring had been piped to the surface close to the road, and here the two Bears and I drove every few days to fill our water bottles and thermos jugs.

Our best friends in Hotevilla were Paul Sewemaenewa, Corn That Has Been Rooted, and his wife, Jeanette, who with their two small children lived in one big room. Paul stood more than six feet tall: big boned, heavy muscled, strong as a horse; but gentle and kind as a child, and humbly devout in his traditional belief. Jeanette was small and meek, forever feeding splinters into the little iron cooking stove, seemingly unmindful of their poverty. Between them existed a faith that had endured years of hardship, and a courtesy that was inspiring to observe.

Paul was a leader of the Eagle Clan. After being immured in the kiva for a long ceremony, he would return to the house to be greeted quietly by his wife. "I thank you for the long concentration and prayers you have made for us, for our people, for everybody throughout the world. May our life be blessed and grow richer for your work. Now I welcome you back to your home."

More than any man I know, Paul was a true Hopi, a dedicated man of peace. When the United States entered World War II, Paul and five other Hopis refused to register for selective service in the Armed Forces and were arrested by the county sheriff who had come from Holbrook at the summons of the agent at Keams Canyon. They were jailed in Holbrook for several days, imprisoned in Prescott for three months, and finally taken to Phoenix to stand trial. Here Paul reaffirmed his Hopi faith.

"With us is our Guardian Spirit whom we promised not to kill any white man that would come to our shores. For we knew our lost white brother, Pahana, would come. If we fought any white man we would fight our own brother, and we do not want our own brother's blood shed on our sacred soil. If we did sign our name and go to war, we might not have a chance to live in the next world. This is our main purpose for not wanting to fight. We are doing this for the Hopi people, not for ourselves."

Paul and his companions were adjudged guilty, evidently on the grounds that they could not be exempted as conscientious objectors because their Hopi belief was not a recognized church or religion. They were sentenced to three years hard labor and taken to the prison camp at Tucson to work in a gang blasting a road up Mount Lemon.

Reinforced by a vision from their Guardian Spirit, the Hopis worked so hard that they were taken off the rock pile to work on farms. This was work they loved, and Paul found time at night to weave belts and sashes which he presented to the men in charge of the prisoners. When he was finally sent home, he found that his sheep had increased to more than a hundred. Then a government agent came, demanding that his flock be reduced. Paul refused to comply. Again he was arrested, stood trial, and was sent back to the prison camp for another year for refusing to give up the sheep that the Creator had given him in answer to his prayers.

While he was away, the Hopi stock reduction was enforced. Half of his flock was taken away. His old mother and his wife, heavy with child, were forced to drive the rest nine miles back home across the desert. On the way Jeanette lost her child. That winter all the remaining sheep had to be killed, for the women were too old and weak to take care of them. So when Paul was finally released, it was to come home to an impoverished family and a wife who had lost her child. Still he could say, "I am glad we have suffered these things, because we were working not only for ourselves, but for all the people in the world; and we are going to follow our life plan and religious teachings."

Now, twenty years later, Paul had another small flock of sheep and an old pickup truck in which he hauled things for other Hopis. It was always breaking down and he had difficulty finding money to pay for repairs. A few months after I met him he lost the sight of one eye because of an infection that was not treated promptly enough at the hospital in Keams Canyon. Despite this, he still wove belts and sashes on a small loom in the corner during the winter.

Paul and Jeanette's two small children, a boy and a girl, loved to visit us in New Oraibi. Everything in the Bears' apartment seemed so new and wonderful!—the clean white dishes, shiny forks and knives, the gas stove, and the refrigerator. Most of all they liked to thumb through magazines to look at the full-color advertisements. Every so often one of them would stop, point at an article, and say proudly in English, "apple," "chair," "car." Sharp and avid to learn, they were not permitted to go to school. They faced the prospect of growing up uneducated in this Space Age, fortified against the Tribal Council, the government, and the white people who had betrayed their father. Paul and Jeanette's point of view was easy to understand.

Although we also had friends and spokesmen on First Mesa, we visited its three villages less often. Hano, Sichomovi, and Walpi especially, were spectacular on their high clifftop and the best known to tourists. Yet to me they seemed the least "typically Hopi." They had always been the first point of contact for whites throughout history, and they were closest to the agency in Keams Canyon which made them susceptible to government influence. Hano itself was not Hopi; it had been settled by refugees from the Rio Grande and the Tewa tongue was still spoken, along with Hopi. Aside from these rational excuses for prejudice, I felt a miasma of defeat and decay clinging about them all. It seemed to permeate every villager, every building. Even the ceremonies seemed imbued with an air of careless abandon. Old Oraibi was frankly dead, an archaeological ruin. This was worse. Here on First Mesa one felt the disease and corruption setting in as the tide of life ebbed away. The survivors lived, like zombies, a meaningless life-in-death. Only in the pottery, for which it was famous, did the last effulgence of life burst into flame—into deep yellow and burnt-orange bowls and vases of exquisite shape, design, and texture. All the women made pottery and one of the best of them was Faye Avachoya, a cheerful little wraith I had met years ago when she was visiting the Rio Grande pueblos. I visited her often.

The fatal blight that had struck First Mesa comprised all the innovations and advantages offered by our own culture. They were condensed in Polacca, a complex of missionary, school, and government buildings at the foot of the mesa. Like New Oraibi which had drained the life out of Old Oraibi, Polacca was draining the life out of Sichomovi, Hano, and Walpi by negating their own inherent center. It was inevitable, of course. But I often wondered if the process of deterioration could have been halted, and the transition to new values made easier by the simple provision of a plaza in these centerless, utility complexes.

5. THE DINOSAUR TRACKS

Of all our spokesmen throughout the villages, Otto Pentiwa in New Oraibi was the funniest—perhaps because like all good comics he played his role straight.

Almost every day we would see him driving down the road in his springless box-wagon behind a scarecrow old nag with flapping eye-blinders. Otto sat erect on the plank seat. He was a middle-aged man whose pudgy flesh rounded out a powerful frame, his dark full-moon face glowing under a tattered cap with its loose ear-flaps flopping up and down like the flapping eye-blinders on his horse.

"There goes Otto," somebody would say.

"Which one?" another would ask.

This was a standard Hopi joke, for Otto and his horse indeed bore a family resemblance.

Pentiwa in English meant "Painting Many Kachina Masks," indicating that he belonged to the Kachina Clan. Its land holdings were out in the desert some miles from town, and during the summer Otto rode out there every day to work his melon patch. Melons of every kind were the Hopis' favorite delicacy. What was better than to come in from the blistering sandy fields and break open a fresh melon, feeling the juice running down a dusty chin and creeping over a parched tongue to a dry throat? A melon packed in sand for months tasted even better in midwinter. It was not unusual to see children, shivering in below-zero cold during a winter dance, avidly attacking a slice of red watermelon given them by a kachina. Otto's melons were admittedly the best and he was generous with them. He drove in late every afternoon with a load, stopping at every house to present one, with a joke and a courtly gesture.

Otto came often to lunch or supper. He sat erect at table, perhaps to prevent his ear-flaps from dangling in his bowl of soup or stew, lifting his spoon high into the air. Here it would remain suspended until he finished his current joke. Then with an odd, quick motion we grew to watch for, it would disappear in a hasty gulp. We loved to have him come, not only because he lived alone and enjoyed a hot meal, but because he was a great deal more than a jokester.

There was a practicing medicine-man in town, but I suspected that in case of his absence or an emergency Otto could serve with dispatch. He knew the centers of the body which controlled man's functions, and how to see what was wrong with any of them by looking through a crystal. There was nothing magical about the crystal, he insisted: it merely objectified the vision of the center which controlled the eyes. Aside from this, he possessed an extraordinary intuition.

I once asked him about this faculty. For answer he took off his tattered cap for once, and patted the top of his head. "You must keep the door open," he said simply.

This *kopavi* or "open door" lay at the crown of his head. It was the soft spot with which a child was born, through which he received his life and communicated with its Giver. For with every breath the soft spot moved up and down with a gentle vibration which was communicated to his Creator. Normally it hardened soon and remained closed until his death, when it opened again for his life to depart. But anyone could learn to keep it open if he tried.

Otto was an invaluable spokesman. White Bear and I at the time were trying to collect material on the complex and esoteric Creation myth, and Otto knew a great deal about the three previous worlds in which man had existed: the name of each; its color and direction; its significant mineral, plant, animal, and bird; and why and how it was destroyed. He taped all this information as casually and unconcernedly as he related tidbits of village gossip between jokes.

What a wonderful story was this Creation myth! It related how mankind had lived successively on these previous worlds, each of which had been destroyed when mankind became wicked, save for a few chosen people who had been safely transplanted to the next. That the Hopis were as familiar with the details of their Creation as we are with our own did not surprise me. What did seem significant was how strongly its meaning possessed them. The guilt of having seen three worlds corrupted by evil; the necessity of living pure and undefiled in this present Fourth World so that, like Paul Sewemaenewa, they might have a chance to live in the future Fifth World—this was the motif that ran through every ceremony and the moral stricture that guided their personal lives. Our own Creation myth of Adam and Eve banished from the Garden of Eden upon the inception of mortal sin was basically the same. Yet for us as individuals its symbolism had worn thin and meaningless; that of the Hopis still comprised a living faith.

Who the Hopis were, whence they had come to this continent, and when, was still an anthropological mystery. They were included in the Uto-Aztecan linguistic group, indicating their relationship to the great racial complex of prehistoric Nahuatl peoples which included the Toltecs and Aztecs of Mexico. It did not surprise me, then, to find in the Toltecan-Aztecan Creation myth a parallel to that of the Hopis.

According to Aztec myth, which in turn derived from the older Toltecs, there were four successive worlds, eras, or suns, each destroyed by a cataclysm. The first was the world of Earth, of dark matter, whose inhabitants were beyond redemption. The second was the world of Air, of spirit destined to become incarnate, its inhabitants being turned into animal forms. The third was that of Fire, from which only the birds escaped. The fourth was the world of Water, from which the fishes arrived. These four worlds were symbolized as a four-square mandala, or quincunx, with the Fifth World as a unifying center. Its symbol was man in whom all the evolutionary movements of the preceding worlds were synthesized. Here then was the first appearance of man and the birth of spirituality by which alone he could progress to future worlds.

The Creation myth as it unfolded that winter engrossed me more and more. Within its dramatic story lay truths common to us all. I began to wonder if the mythical previous worlds were psychologically equated to the physical and psychical centers of the human body, each of which functioned predominantly at successive stages of mankind's existence. Was man's Road of Life through all these worlds or stages of existence a dramatic parable of his evolutionary development? What in reality was the dread evil, the mortal sin that the ancestral Hopis, like Adam and Eve, had committed?

It was not my task to read into Hopi mythology these implicit, universal meanings. The expressed purpose of my work was to induce our Hopi spokesmen to speak for themselves and their people, literally and truthfully as possible. Nevertheless, such implications were too apparent to be ignored and I pondered over these questions during the lonely winter at Pumpkin Seed Point. Then, towards spring, occurred an incident that curiously condensed all the ramifications of my questioning in one unique image.

Another Tribal Council meeting was held in the Mormon church outside Moencopi, fifty miles west. White Bear and I drove over to attend it. The morning was warm and sunny. Not a cloud marred the turquoise sky. The first touch of spring was in the air.

The road snaked down Third Mesa, crawled across the sandy

plain, and crept up to the high, level plateau stretching westward to the forested mountains that flanked Grand Canyon. This was Navajo country now. A barren waste spotted with clumps of grass chewed down to their roots by sparse flocks of Navajo sheep. Occasionally a lone horseman plodding to a mud-plastered hogan, isolated and lonely in empty space. A vast flatland that still boasted height and depth—in far-off pillared buttes standing like the stelae of a vanished ancient world, and in the great intaglio of Coal Canyon eroded into the same fantastic shapes.

Moencopi, the most distant Hopi village, lay down in a great wash whose banks, soft and fine as sand dunes, gave miraculous birth each year to stalks of corn and patches of melons. Above it, just off the road, stood the Mormon missionary church. It was already crowded with people waiting not so much for the meeting as for the lunch that was soon served in a house in the upper village. Among them were several Navajos, of course.

"Them people are like buzzards. They can smell a dinner a hundred miles away!" someone said. The Navajos didn't mind. They packed away in their hard flat bellies chunks of mutton, potatoes, carrots, *piki*, store cake with pink icing, peach pie, and strong black coffee. Then we went back to the church and the meeting began.

Sight of those tall, virile, and arrogant Navajos had upset White Bear. The droning, pointless, and ineffective voices of the Tribal Council speakers bothered me still more. It was all very boring, really. We slipped out the door, deciding to call upon a Hopi who lived up Shalako Canyon.

Due west lay Tuba City, a scatter of houses in which lived a few government employees, traders, and missionaries to the Navajos. Here we turned north on the road to Monument Valley. It threaded a long, narrow valley flanked on each side by craggy volcanic cliffs. High on those to the right nestled the eyries of eagles immemorially captured by the Hopis for the Niman Kachina ceremony. Below the cliffs stood Owaventewa, Where Everyone Writes On a Rock. There were a dozen of these great Inscription Rocks, each covered with a maze of petroglyphs hacked into the brown, burnt stone. They were the clan signatures of generations of Hopi initiates who had passed by here on their pilgrimage to the secret salt cave in the depths of Grand Canyon whose eastward wall rose far to the left.

In a little while White Bear turned left on a faintly marked wagon road that crawled up a desolate, narrow canyon of hard, brown, volcanic tufa. Unable to drive farther, we left the car and walked farther up the rising canyon. Its tortuously eroded walls assumed queerer and queerer shapes. The strata no longer lay horizontal, one upon the other. They had been bent to stand vertically and then gently folded over to form great curves and arches, leaving below mosaics of small pebbles and agates.

Soon we came upon a stream that had been dammed to form a crude reservoir. It was filled with a growth of tules and cattails, and was surrounded by living green. What a beautiful, hidden oasis in this parched-rock, desert valley during the blistering heat of summer! It was beautiful now even in early spring.

The pool was an enchanted spot as well as an enchanting one. No one drank water from it. White Bear told me why. One day a Hopi man living near here had seen a woman emerging wet and naked from the tules. She came up to him smiling, so beautiful and appealing that he "forgot his will" and allowed her to seduce him. Afterward, she waded back into the tules and disappeared beneath the water, beckoning to him to follow her. Then the man realized she was a water serpent. Horrified, he rushed home to tell his family. It was too late. He died "four later"—four days, months, or years. Since that time most Hopis have avoided this isolated spot. Besides, it lay in an area now claimed by the encroaching Navajos.

Only one man lived here, a lonely Hopi recluse who stoutly defended himself against government edict and Navajo encroachment. He was the man we were seeking, and we finally came to his house at the head of the canyon. It was a small hut enclosed within a corral of stout timbers. Gate and door were securely barred and locked. Disappointed at not finding him, we turned and began walking back.

Then we saw them. They lay at our feet, imprinted in the smooth volcanic rock floor of the canyon. A litter of huge, deeply imbedded, birdlike tracks, each showing the clear imprint of four outspread toes. Dinosaur tracks.

There was no mistaking them. Others had been seen on the desert toward Oraibi before they were uprooted by road construction crews. Some of them just off the highway near Moencopi were still protected by a wire fence, and one of them was tidily mounted in the museum outside of Flagstaff. It was identified as belonging to the species *chirotherium* which existed 200 million years ago.

It was one thing to see this single specimen in the museum, but something else to suddenly see so many of them here as if these monsters had just lifted their feet and walked off into that vast, sunlit valley spreading out below us. Time was suddenly and unaccountably compressed into a dimensionless, ever-living *now*. The sun still beat down with glaring brightness as it always had. The stars had not moved out of their immortal pattern in the skies of night. Threads of rain were still unraveling the great maze of Grand Canyon behind us. Nothing had changed here since the day this hard volcanic rock was still viscous mud beneath

61

the steps of these gigantic monsters.

Yet something had removed them from our sight. What it was no man knew. These dinosaurs were living lords of their earth, breathing forth a power greater than government edict, trampling all beneath their armed might. Yet their whole species had been obliterated in order that a speck of green scum in that fetid pool might form into the flesh and blood of a puny, cringing, and defenseless mammal, and so endure as man: a species unremarkable save that, despite his many faults and mistakes, he still acknowledged the mysterious laws of his Creation; that he still, through the alluring temptations that beckoned from his past, through all his superstitions and rationalizations, stubbornly perpetuated a queer, blind belief in the final triumph of moral right over armed might, of love and brotherhood over hate and factional division.

To that enduring mystery of his being no man could give proper shape or form or word. Yet it seemed perfectly expressed, as commandments once engraved on another stone, in those gigantic four-toed tracks imprinted in the rock before us. I felt I knew now the meaning of the Hopis' Creation myth, the mortal sin we dare not commit, and the one abiding virtue that insures our slow progression along the evolutionary Road of Life. What a difference was revealed between the Indian and the white relationship with nature!

6. TWO VIEWS OF NATURE

Contemporary Hopi, Zuni, and many other Indian tribes, as well as the prehistoric Toltecs and Aztecs, believe in the myth that they lived successively in three previous worlds before coming to this one. What root race of mankind these Indians of Mesoamerica belonged to, what vanished or still-existent continent they came from, when, and how, no one knows. Their origin is lost in a time that is being continually pushed back to the edge of the one great mystery of life. Yet these documentary questions need not trouble us. The great myth of their Emergence, as the Hopis most aptly call their arrival upon this continent, is the dramatized story of the emergence of consciousness from the great pool of the unconscious—the evolution of that consciousness of object and self which has enabled man alone to distinguish himself from the rest of nature. It is one of the great awakenings along the Road of Life. By it man gives the world its objective existence and so partakes himself in the process of Creation.

How wonderful it must have been, this ancient and unknown America, this new and promising Fourth World, when man first saw it through Indian eyes! So glistening fresh with the dawn's dew on it. So pristinely pure, so virginly naked in its beauty. How enchantingly diverse the land was with range upon range of snowcapped mountains, shimmering deserts lying below the level of the seas that gnawed at its shores, arctic tundras merging into illimitable plains of waving grass, rising into high-level plateaus, and sinking again into fetid tropical jungles. All teaming with life in every form, tiny plants and dense forests, birds, reptiles and insects, and countless animals of many unique species now extinct, like the buffalo whose vast herds blackened the tawny plains. A land with its own great spirit of place, its own brooding destiny hovering over it with invisible wings.

The Hopis, like other branches of their race, knew themselves as privileged newcomers to this great new world. So upon their arrival they first asked permission to live upon it from its guardian spirit and protector. The spirit gave his permission, telling them, however, that they were not free to wander over it rampantly, using it as they wished. They were to make ordered migrations, north, south, east, and west, to the four *pasos* where the land met the sea, before settling in the place prescribed for their permanent home. There they were to establish those annual ceremonies which would recapitulate their wanderings and reclaim the land for its Creator.

The meaning of the myth is clear. The emergence of consciousness does not set man entirely free. He is still obligated to the dictates of the unconscious which embodies all his primordial past. He may travel to the limits of his mind and will, but he must always observe those thaumaturgical rites which acknowledge his arising from the one great origin of all life and which keep him whole.

Such a tradition, like many other versions of its kind, marked the relationship of the Hopis to the land. If the directional peaks and boundary rivers to their tribal homeland were stained with the blood of a virginal youth and maiden, the memory of their sacrifices was perpetuated through uncounted generations by male-and-female prayer-feathers planted on ceremonial altars to remind all men of the sacred foundation of their tenure. The land was not tangible property to be owned, divided, and alienated at will. It was their Mother Earth from which they were born, on whose breast they were suckled, and to whose womb they were returned in a prenatal posture at death.

The earth-mother had many children other than man: the stem of long wild grass that developed into a stalk of maize, the lofty spruce, all the birds of the air, the beasts of plain and forest, the insect and the ant. They too had equal rights to life. They supplied the needs of man, but they were not sacrificed ruthlessly and wantonly. A deer was killed only after obtaining his ceremonial assent to the killing that enabled all life to endure in its ordered pattern. Eagles were needed for their down and feathers. But first their heads were washed to signify their adoption into the tribe. Then their lives were snuffed out (bloodlessly) with a blanket and their stripped bodies were carried to an eagle burying ground. The tall and stately spruce furnished its trunk, branches, and tufts of needles. The tree was asked also to consent to its necessary sacrifice, and it was given a special drink so that it would not feel pain from the axe. How remarkably similar these still-observed rituals were among widely separated tribes throughout the Southwest and Mexico.

They may seem curiously sentimental to those of us who are accustomed to think of matter and spirit as antithetical. Yet they conform to the common belief, held by all American Indian tribes, in a mysterious force or dynamic energy, an impersonal spirit of life, pervading and uniting every entity in nature—the living stone, the great breathing mountain, plant, bird, animal, and man. It was the *orenda* of the Iroquois, the *maxpe* of the Crows, the Sioux *mahopa,* the Algonquin *manito.* And their belief is validated by the mystery teachings of the East which assert that everything is alive to the degree in which its consciousness is dormant, sleeping, or awakened. Hence the Indians did not set themselves apart from all other physical forms of life. They regarded themselves as a part of one living whole.

Each entity in nature, then, possessed not only an outer physical form but an inner spiritual force. Man was free to utilize the fleshly form for his own bodily needs. But he was ever aware that its spiritual component remained alive as a source of psychical energy which could be invoked to manifest its benign powers for his need.

These spiritual components the Hopis called kachinas, "respected spirits," and they are invoked each year still. Spirits of plant, bird, animal, and human beings who have died; of all the invisible forces of life, they manifest themselves in the physical forms of men wearing masks imbued with the powers of the spirits they represent. So they come dancing into the plazas, uttering their own strange cries, singing from dawn to sunset.

Such a ceremony is a profound mystery play which if produced in Europe would draw thousands of Americans in an annual and fashionable pilgrimage. Still there are pitifully few people here who appreciate it as a superlative, indigenous art form whose anthropomorphic masks, stylistic dancing, and subtle rhythms of song have no equal throughout the world. This superficial artistic consideration, however, is validated by the basic truth and meaning of the kachina. However unique and complex it may seem, the Hopis have created with it a form for the everlasting formless; a living symbol for that universal spirit which embodies all matter; and which speaks to us, as only the spirit can speak, through the intuitive perception of our own faith in the one enduring mystery of life.

This primitive, animistic view of nature, as we are accustomed to regard it, emerges in true perspective only when we compare it to our own Euro-American view of nature.

It too, like the Indians', springs from a long religious tradition. One reads in the first chapter of Genesis, in our Judaic-Christian Bible, that man was created in God's own image and divinely commanded to subdue the earth. The connotations of the word "subdue" cannot be lightly disregarded. For in this view of the dualism of man and nature perhaps lies the real beginning of human tragedy in the Western Hemisphere. The Christian-European white race, from its first discovery of this pristine New World of the red race, regarded it as one vast new treasure house of inanimate nature that existed solely to be exploited for the material welfare of man. So one sees the Spanish spearheads of conquest thrusting into Peru under Pizarro and into Mexico under Cortés. And one watches closer home the Anglo course of empire sweeping like an engulfing tide across our own America from sea to sea. How little time it took to subdue the continent! It was a rapacious achievement whose scope and speed have not been equalled in all history. Year by year, and mile by mile westward, the white conquerors leveled whole forests under the axe, plowed under the grasslands, dammed and drained the rivers, gutted the mountains for gold and silver, and divided and sold and resold the land itself. Accompanying all this destruction was the extermination of birds and beasts, another aspect of nature inimical to man. Not for sport or profit alone, but to indulge a wanton lust for killing that wiped out vast herds of buffalo at a time, leaving tens of thousands of carcasses piled in a heap to rot in the sun.

The results of our savage onslaught against nature are now all too evident. We have so denuded the grasslands and forested mountains that the topsoil is washing down the drain into the sea. The underground water level is lowering so rapidly that we are being forced to develop means for purifying sea water for our use. The very air we breathe is becoming dangerously toxic in all our large cities, and radioactive fallout from our latest technological triumph is laying to waste wide swaths around the whole planet.

Yet it is not enough to have subdued a continent and exhausted its natural resources. There still remains a vast domain of untouched nature in the universe—the other planets in outer

67

space; and to reach them we have already committed ourselves to exploratory voyages. Is it naive to ask if the purpose of our national space effort is to subdue, colonize, and exploit them also for our material ends? Or is it simply because we are caught in the maelstrom of a technology that cannot be stopped?

In the field of inquiry which these questions pose lies the human tragedy of America, both ours and the Indians'. For accompanying the rapacious destruction of nature from the very start was the virtual extermination of all Indians. These savages, as often viewed by the whites, were not human beings. Like wild beasts which possessed neither souls nor reason, they too were an inalienable part of that vast body of nature inimical to man and hence an embodiment of evil.

History has documented the tragic massacre of tribe after tribe across the continent throughout our "Century of Dishonor" far beyond the need to comment on it here. But when at last the holocaust was over, there were left throughout all the land scarcely 200,000 Indians penned up in ever-dwindling Reservations.

Chief Seattle, for whom one of our cities was named, spoke the epitaph of his race:

"We are two distinct races with separate origins and separate destinies. To us the ashes of our ancestors are sacred and their resting place is hallowed ground. You wander far from the graves of your ancestors and seemingly without regret. . . .

"But why should I mourn at the untimely fate of my people? Tribe follows tribe, and nation follows nation, and regret is useless. . . .

"But when the last red man shall have become a myth among the white men . . . when your children's children think themselves alone in the field, the store, upon the highway, or in the silence of the pathless woods, they will not be alone. In all the earth there is no place dedicated to solitude. At night when the streets of your cities are silent and you think them deserted, they will throng with the returning hosts that once filled them and still love this beautiful land. The white man will never be alone.

"Let him be just and deal kindly with my people, for the dead are not powerless. Dead?—I say. There is no death. Only a change of worlds."

These noble sentiments did not mitigate the cumulative effects of this fateful disaster upon us all. They perceptively forewarned us of the ghosts that now stalk our streets, the burden of guilt under which our national conscience is beginning to stagger, and the racial prejudice against people of all colored skins engendered in us. Yet when we view the decimation of the red race within the context of white belief, our retrospective compassion loses much of its emotional intensity. For the tragedy was not only the Indian's, but the white man's too.

Man was not created apart from nature, as he thought, but out of nature whose unconscious forces and instinctual drives still swayed him. So we, the whites, while subduing nature, also tried to subdue the aspects of nature within ourselves—the secret and shameful desires of "natural" man, the appetites of the flesh, all the instincts so incompatible and hostile to the mores of rational man. Our own minds and bodies became the battleground of man against nature, man against God, and man against himself, divided into two warring selves: reason and instinct, the conscious and the unconscious.

The outcome was never in doubt, for the white newcomers

had committed the one sin against which the great spirit, Masaw, had warned the arriving Hopis. They had cut themselves off from the roots of life.

With the phenomenal rise and spread of Western civilization we have now become the richest materialistic nation that ever existed on this planet. The monstrous paradox is that while we have created untold benefits for all mankind, we have impoverished ourselves spiritually in the process. In achieving what seems to be a complete triumph over nature, we have established a machine-made society so utterly devitalized that it is anticipating the synthetic creation of life within a laboratory test tube. What could be more reasonable, then, than to enthrone the machine as its deity?

The refutation is expresssed by nature itself—that one great unity of all Creation, imbued with one consciousness and infused with one power, of which everything in the universe is an embodied part. Everything is alive, differentiated not in kind but only in the degree of sentiency with which it reflects this all-pervading life in the ascent from mineral to man. The life of the whole is an unconscious process illuminated by consciousness. But pragmatic consciousness is limited. It lights up not the whole, but only a fact-section of it. Hence man's viewpoint is partial. He selects only that part which seems useful to him, ignoring and disowning the rest.

That part, to rational Western man, has been constantly decreasing. It has been successively reduced to that small segment of humanity comprising the white race, to Western Europeans, and now with excessive nationalism largely to American-dominated political entities. The trend is against the evolutionary tide of nature, by which he must constantly extend his frontiers of consciousness. Not only to include all the races of humanity, primitive as they may be; but to establish a living relationship with the animal kingdom, the plant kingdom, that of the living earth itself, and finally the whole of the universe of which he is in reality an enfranchised citizen.

These then are the two pictures broadly outlined by our opposite views of nature. The extrovert view generally held by white Europeans and the introvert view traditional to the colored races of the Far East as well as to Indian America are complementary sides of the same coin. If rational man came from nature in order to stand apart and see nature objectively, nature came to itself in man in order to see itself subjectively. The comprehensive view, it would seem, must come from a perspective that includes both instinct and reason. How are we to reach it?

This problem of means and ends seems strangely acute to a man not too well informed of current events by the Village Crier here in New Oraibi. Like many undeveloped countries it stands on the perimeters of two worlds, owing full allegiance to neither. Which way is New Oraibi to turn? It cannot remain in the primitive Hopi past. Nor can it go forward into a technological future so threateningly sterile. Western civilization also stands at a major crossroads. Its hard-won consciousness cannot sink into the unconscious. Nor can it persist in its rational, willful alienation from life. We both have reached an impasse that the H-bomb may well solve for us.

The Village Crier does not, of course, keep us posted every morning on the steadily rising fallout rate. But almost daily we are informed of the widespread trend of Hopi prophecy. It suggests a way out of our present tragic dilemma. Long, long ago when the Third World became evil and sterile, preparations were made for mankind's Emergence to a new Fourth World. The people were told simply to keep open the *kopavi* at the crown of the head.

71

Through this "open door" to the Creator they would receive guidance to the shore of their new world and then to their homeland during their fourfold, continental migrations. So it was they were led by the voice of their guardian spirit, by kachinas, by a star—by all the voices, shapes, and symbols through which intuition speaks to our inner selves.

Today, says Hopi prophecy, mankind is ready for an Emergence to a new Fifth World. Once again we must strive to keep open the door. Through it we will hear a new voice, glimpse a new star to follow. It will be Sasquasohuh, the Blue Star, far off and invisible yet, but to appear soon. We will know when it appears, for Sasquasohuh, the Blue Star Kachina, its manifested spirit, will dance in the *kisonvi* for the first time.

We whites also stand on the threshold of a new epoch in the evolution of mankind. Nearly 2,000 years ago a new star appeared to the wisest of our kind also. It led them to the manifested spirit of a new urge within man, to a new faith that for century after century embodied all our needs. The meaning of Christianity is not antiquated today, but it has been distorted into moral precepts by a church community which has deteriorated into a social-political institution. Excessively rational man now reads its mythical parables as mere historical events, substituting knowledge for faith, forgetting that the seat of faith is not consciousness but the unconscious. It is from this only source of religious experience that we too must look for the appearance of a new star, a new symbol to rejuvenate our faith in life itself.

By it we must chart our course through the great, unknown interstellar spaces within us, the new world of the future. Even modern science, in its reduction of material units to smaller and smaller size, recognizes that matter does not exist. It consists only of electrical fields unified by the attraction of their opposite polarities—the invisible kachina forces envisaged by our generally ignored Hopis. Is it impossible to concede that beneficent psychical energy may be evoked from them as well as the destructive physical energy released by the hydrogen bomb?

So it seems to me as I lie here in the little house below Pumpkin Seed Point that our two views, ours and the Hopis', are not too divergent after all. Extravagantly pessimistic and suspicious of each other as we are, we are both curiously imbued with the same unfounded belief in the mysterious continuity of life that will raise us to a level on which we will see reconciled in fuller perspective the opposite and complementary sides of our common coin. Already we have come a long way from the speck of green scum in that fetid pool beside the dinosaur tracks imprinted on the rocky floor of Shalako Canyon. But the journey ahead, like that behind us, lies through the subjective realm of time and love; there is no short cut through outer space by mechanical travel.

7. THE SPRING IN THE SHADOWS

White Bear and I had climbed up the old trail to Oraibi and were walking across the mesa when we were suddenly halted by the sight of a man at the edge of the cliffs. He was standing with his right arm upraised, his hand resting against the cliff wall. His body was bare to the waist and glowed red-brown in the sunlight. His long fall of grey hair, held by a headband of faded red silk and cut into square bangs that hung below his ears, obscured his face. Far below, the desert lay empty in the unbroken, heavy silence of hot noon. Yet the man's posture of rapt attention seemed curiously familiar.

"That's the man you saw in your dream!" I said abruptly.

White Bear had dreamed some nights before that he was standing on a cliff edge, watching a man pulling on a string tied to a rock overhead. At each pull on the string the rock began to talk, relating happenings that had occurred centuries ago.

"So this is how you get your knowledge of the past?" White Bear had asked him.

"Yes," answered the man. "All these stones have voices. Just find yourself a rock and pull the string. You too have been given the power to hear."

That was how I met John Lansa of Old Oraibi. There was no nonsense about him. Despite his seventy years, he was mentally alert, quick-moving, and tireless. He could race up a steep, rocky slope sure-footed as a cat, leaving far younger men to pant and stumble behind him. This inexhaustible physical energy came from herding the small band of sheep that furnished his livelihood. He would take them out into the desert for days at a time, living only on a few rolls of *piki,* the paper-thin cornbread that is the Hopi's staff of life, and a bit of dried meat or jerky.

His psychic energy also was constantly replenished by these long reflective periods alone under sun and stars. He was invariably cheerful and good-natured, down-to-earth and practical in all things. His devout belief in his people's traditional ceremonialism reflected this practicality. He regarded his life and livelihood as gifts of his Creator; in return for them he meticulously observed not only every ritual left to him, but the divine injunction of thankful prayers and good thoughts at all times.

His wife Myna, sharp-eyed and resolute, was no less remarkably integrated. In her custody Chief Tawkwaptiwa had left the sacred tablet given to the Bear Clan when it arrived on this Fourth World. This was in accord with tradition, for Myna was of the Parrot Clan, symbolic mother of the Hopis, as the Bear Clan was regarded as their father. She brought out this tablet from its hiding place one day for us to see it. The stone was about ten inches long and eight inches wide, of a dull gray color with intrusive blotches of rose. It was engraved on one side with the figures of six men enclosed within a double rectangle, and marked on the other side with a maze of symbols. All these markings John readily interpreted for us. The stone tablet, he said, spoke with a clear voice.

His quick interpretation confirmed his resemblance to the man in White Bear's dream who had been engaged in making the rock talk. John could do just that. He had the ability to read like a newspaper all the pictographs, petroglyphs, symbols, and clan signatures engraved on rocks, boulders, and cliff walls everywhere. It was more than a developed ability: an intuitive faculty he seemed to have been born with.

Not only were the cliffs below Oraibi covered with markings, but rocks in every canyon for miles around. Indeed, they were to be found throughout all the Southwest, Mexico, and Guatemala. The vast amount and extent of this "rock writing" seemed to me to warrant a comprehensive study. If some of it can be dismissed as recent scribbling and doodling, there are also symbols identical with those found in Asia and Africa carved a thousand years ago or more. I use the word "writing" in its widest, nonacademic sense. Crude as it was, and composed of abstract symbols, pictographs, petroglyphs, and simple figures drawn from nature, it comprised a pictorial language whose principal characters were similar wherever found.

John's faculty was an invaluable help to us, for we were then engaged in collecting the legends and tracing the routes of the prehistoric migrations of various clans. We took him to the abandoned Great Pueblos of Chaco Canyon in New Mexico, to the cliff-dwellings of Mesa Verde, Colorado, and to innumerable other ruins not yet identitfied or excavated throughout Arizona. Somewhere around them John always found rock writing and could "pull the string," deciphering their meanings—signatures of clans which once had occupied the ruins, a depicted incident which confirmed an oral legend, and symbols of religious significance readily equated with contemporary rituals.

John roomed with me in the motel at which we spent the night, and was up before dawn to greet the rising sun. His prayer followed the ancient pattern and it was beautiful to watch. He would stand in the open doorway facing east, barefooted and stripped to the waist. The first deep yellow to appear in the sky was sun pollen. Four times he would scrape it off the horizon with his cupped hand and put it in his mouth. This fed his body. As the sun began to rise, he breathed deeply four times to cleanse his heart and his insides. Then four times he spread the first rays of the sun over himself from head to feet, clothing himself in its power. Finally as he faced the sun, now fully risen, he reminded himself to keep his countenance full, benign, and as cheerful as the face of the sun. At these times his slim, erect, red-brown body reminded me of the meaning of his name, "Lance"; it was as straight and clean as a shaft of the sun itself.

John was a member of the important Badger Clan which controlled the Niman Kachina ceremony. This was the first of the three major summer ceremonies which symbolically harvested the prayers and life patterns planted during the three winter ceremonies, and we were particularly eager to visit one of the sacred shrines which figured in its rituals.

Kisiwu, The Spring in the Shadows, served many functions. To it were carried the *pahos* or prayer-feathers made in the kivas. From the great spruce trees around it were brought back the branches and twigs worn by the dancing kachinas and the two small spruce trees which were planted in the plaza on the night before the dance. Here in an unexcavated ruin the Badger Clan had lived before coming to Oraibi centuries ago. Here too was the home of Chowilawu, the deity of the Badger Clan, and his sister, Angwusnasomtaqa, the Crow Mother, of the Kachina Clan. It was a sacred, mysterious place, and many strange tales were told about it.

John had no reluctance in taking us to it. Early one morning the four of us—the two Bears, John, and myself—piled in the car and started out. It was a difficult trip of perhaps fifty miles—east to the remote trading post of Piñon, then northeast across Black Mesa toward Monument Valley. From here to Kayenta there was no settlement, no trading post, no road across this wild and desolate upland desert. The rutted dirt road climbed up one tortuous mud hill after another, snaked down into a sandy wash, then emerged into a long narrow valley stretching between two low ranges covered with piñon. By this time there was no road at all, simply wagon ruts cut into the soft mud during spring rains and hardening into deep trenches with high centers over which it was difficult for a car to pass. Far off loomed a solitary Navajo hogan with a pickup moored beside it in a sea of sage. A hawk hung motionless from the hot, steel shield of the sky. There was no other sign of life.

It was fortunate that John was guiding us; he knew every step of the way. Years ago, before the observance of Niman Kachina was given up at Oraibi, he had made the annual pilgrimage twelve times. It was always made on foot, according to custom, and no salt was eaten during the long trip. As the leader or "message carrier," John was accompanied by two younger men on guard against any evil manifestations that might hinder their trip, always fraught with spiritual danger. The messages they carried to Kisiwu were *pahos* or prayer-feathers made by the men immured in the kiva. There were many of them of different kinds: small feathers of eagle down attached to a short length of string woven from native cotton, or beautiful and intricate male-and-female *pahos* contrived of many symbolic components.

Shortly before noon we left the car at the foot of a long, rocky hogback covered with spruce and piñon, and began climbing the narrow trail leading up to the escarpment to Kisiwu on top. John led the way, climbing springily as a goat, while I panted behind him. The two Bears followed far in the rear. Suddenly John stopped on a narrow ledge and instructed me to wait.

He went on a few yards, then stopped to take off his moccasins, shirt, pants, and headband. For a moment he stood slimly erect, beads of sweat glistening on his brown body. Then from the little buckskin sack suspended from a thong looped around his throat he sprinkled a pinch of cornmeal on the ground and gave a loud call to the spirits of Kisiwu above. This he repeated three times as he slowly climbed upward to finally offer his prayers in front of a cave high above. Then he motioned for me to join him.

Kisiwu was indeed a spring in the shadows. The spring itself was in the cave, the water oozing out of the rocky walls and forming a deep cold pool at the bottom. The front of the cave had been recently walled with stone, evidently to prevent Navajo sheep from polluting the sacred pool. The dampness of the overhanging roof, said John, was an indication of how much moisture would come during the year. Everywhere inside—planted on every ledge and thrust into every cranny—were the prayer-feathers carried here on countless pilgrimages. Yet they were not planted indiscriminately. The order and position governing their planting determined in what direction, how far, and with what power their prayers would carry.

Nor was there ever any doubt as to how the spirits had answered their prayers. The three message carriers would enter the cave again before returning home and find an eloquent answer in the condition of the prayer-feathers. Some would be still standing straight and firm, their color dulled, indicating that they had drawn moisture. For these John would be thankful. But other carefully planted *pahos* would be disarranged, knocked down and scattered in all directions, showing that the men in the kiva who had made them were impure of thought. Then it was incumbent upon John to identify these *pahos* so that upon his return home he could instruct their makers to concentrate more deeply and pray that their weaknesses would not bring hard times to their people.

Meanwhile the three men making the pilgrimage would climb to a great spruce tree. *"Salavi,"* John would address it respectfully, "we have come to get your leaves to use for our clothes. Please come with us." Blessing the tree and planting a prayer-feather at its foot, the men would then cut down two small trees, a male and a female, and armloads of twigs and branches. These they would bundle on their backs to carry home.

"Salavi, the spruce, you must know," explained John, "has the most powerful magnetic force of all trees, the power to bring clouds and moisture. *Salavi* is the *chochokpi,* the throne for the clouds.

That is what we say. For its branches swing outward and upward, and these arms are *chochokpi,* where the clouds rest. When we take the branches of the spruce we are harvesting, just as we will harvest our corn which will grow from the rain the clouds bring. So it is the spirits of the spruce, the clouds, and the rain who give this life to us, you understand, and these are the spirits who accompany us back home to take part in our ceremony. That is why I say to the kiva chief when I return, 'We have all come.' And that is why he says, 'Enter our kiva, all of you. You are all welcome'."

How quiet and peaceful it was at this ancient, sacred shrine impregnated for so many generations by a people's prayers and hopes for moisture in this barren desert. Yet soon after the two Bears had come panting up the trail, the silence was broken by a sudden high-pitched yell. We jumped to our feet, ran up the trail, and looked down the steep precipice. A tiny figure on horseback was lashing his mount toward a hogan nearby. At his shout several other tiny figures emerged from the doorway and stood looking up in our direction.

"Navajos!" spat John. "We go!"

He ran down the trail, flung on his clothes and headband. We followed him down to the hogan. It was built in the traditional Navajo pattern: octagonal in shape with the door facing east, its log walls plastered with adobe. It evidently housed several families, the nucleus of a remote clan, from the number of men, women, and children gathered in front. John talked rapidly in Navajo. When he finished, the boy jumped on his horse and galloped away. Then we followed an old Navajo into the hogan.

It was large and comfortable, as they all are, warm in winter and cool in summer. The construction of its roof, with interlaced logs and slim poles of red cedar, was exquisite. In the center of the dirt floor a small fire was going, the smoke escaping through a hole in the roof. Around the walls were spread blankets and sheepskins. Close to the door stood a wooden packing box containing groceries and cooking utensils. They were few and simple, for the usual diet of most Navajos was restricted to strong black coffee sweetened with sugar, fried bread, and mutton. Extra clothes were neatly folded over a spruce pole suspended by ropes from the ceiling.

The old Navajo man seated himself opposite the door. On one side of him sat a few other men, and on the other side sat John, the two Bears, and myself. The women and children crouched down on each side of the door. We sat waiting in silence for the men being brought by the boy on horseback.

"They coming soon," said John tersely. He showed no anger; merely a taut sternness that forbade questioning.

Despite its simple outlines, the hogan exuded a warmth and richness that reflected its brilliant, barbaric colors. The blankets spread on the floor were bold and striking of design and richly colored with native dyes. The shirts of the men, worn tail out over their threadbare Levi trousers, were orange and crimson. The women were dressed in equally bright velveteen blouses of purple and dark green, and voluminous pleated gingham skirts bulging out from a half dozen petticoats. All wore the traditional, ankle-high, Navajo moccasins buttoned by silver *conchos*. Each Navajo was loaded with jewelry—chunk-turquoise bracelets, necklaces, and ear pendants; no matter how poor a Navajo was, he always managed this display of silver and turquoise.

Familiar as these hogans were to me from boyhood they reminded me of the *yurts* on the steppes of Mongolia so often pictured by a painter friend, Leon Gaspard, who knew them well. There was the same Asiatic color key, the same feeling of isolated remoteness; and in the faces and the dark eyes of the people too one saw this wildness, this far remoteness. One could readily believe the ethnological assertion that these Navajos were a Mongolian stock who had crossed from Asia to America over Bering Strait, arriving here but a few centuries ago. The Hopis themselves tell of their coming—wild, barbaric strangers dressed only in the skins of wild animals, having no homes, knowing nothing of corn, and begging to be taught the rudiments of Hopi civilization. Little wonder that the Hopis resented them as intruding strangers.

The men we had been waiting for arrived, and the talk began.

John wasted no words. The spring above was a sacred Hopi shrine. It was being polluted by the sheep belonging to these Navajos. Why?

One of the men laughed. What proof did he have for this wild assertion?

"Tracks. I trailed them to the spring. I will show you the tracks if you have no eyes to see." He gave details of the route of their passage. He described the locations of other nearby springs and waterholes where they might have been taken. But these Navajos were too lazy to walk that far. So they let their sheep pollute this sacred Hopi spring. Why?

The old Navajo assented with a nod. The younger one, having lost face, became angry and boldly fingered the knife in its sheath at his waist. John thrust out his arm and forefinger, pointing directly at his opponent. No Navajo likes to be pointed at; and this finger and long arm, backed by two merciless black eyes, had the effect of a gun barrel on the man. He squirmed to one side, scowling.

"Who is to say this is not our land?" the old Navajo asked gently. "Our Tribal Council has not told us. No one has told us. We have been here many years. More of us are coming."

This simple statement by an old, unlettered man in a remote hogan eloquently condensed the whole complex problem of the

Hopi-Navajo land dispute soon to be aired in court. One saw at a glance its swiftly unrolling history. The gentle, village Hopis immemorially settled on their land. The coming of the wild, nomadic Tavasuh, the Head-Pounders, as the Hopis called them, because they killed an enemy by pounding his head with a rock. Then the ever-increasing encroachment of Navajos on Hopi land. In vain the national government prescribed a Hopi Reservation of 4,000 square miles within the immense Navajo Reservation of 25,000 square miles. The Navajos kept coming, 80,000 of them now, squeezing 5,000 Hopis within their villages and sparse cornfields.

What could keep them out? Where else were they to go? Simple, unlearned semi-nomads without homes, following their sheep in search of grass, building a hogan here and there in a trackless, barren wilderness like these families here before us. But a proud, arrogant, and extroverted people whose adaptability knew no bounds. If it were true that the Hopis had taught them how to weave blankets, lay ritual sandpaintings, and fashion jewelry of silver and turquoise, it was also true that the Navajos had raised all these arts to an epitome of perfection. No other blanket matches the Navajo in its superb weave, color, and stylistic design. No other sandpainting achieves the high art and profound meaning than that of the Navajo. Nor is the exquisite Navajo turquoise and silverwork equalled by the best of modern designers.

"Tavasuh! They lie, they steal, they cheat! How evil they are, having many wives apiece to fill the world with children! No wonder the government is powerless against them!"

One could sympathize with the Hopis too in their obsessive hate of everything Navajo. Yet it was difficult to understand their strange reluctance for several centuries to assert their own inalienable rights. It seemed their destiny to submit docilely to dominance and destruction. One kept reminding himself that the word *hopi* means *peace*; and that these People of Peace, by the divine injunction of their faith, have not been permitted to raise a hand in self-defense. Introverted and introspective, sunk deep in the cabalistic maze of their intricate ceremonialism, they seemed like a strange religious cult which had inhibited all life for ritual. A ritualism so profound, however, that even the Navajos respected its power.

So one saw expressed here in this remote hogan not only the conflict between the swiftly growing, extroverted Navajos and the dwindling, introverted Hopis, but the immemorial conflict expressed in national terms throughout the world. It is always a salutory lesson to be reminded that one does not have to seek far, and in too broad terms, to find the problem confronting us all.

John was now thundering invectives with righteous anger. "Chowilawu is the deity of my Badger Clan. He lives up there in our shrine that you pollute. I would have you know how powerful he is. We make four calls for him. At the last call he is in our kiva. He travels that fast through the air. Do you know what power he has? *Tamochpolo,* the power to draw up the muscles back of the knee and so make a man lame, that is what he has! Do you know who his sister is, who lives with him? You have seen her! Angwusnasomtaqa, our Crow Mother, mother of our kachinas. You have seen her, I tell you! Look out the door. See that crow watching you. Ai! Ai! Ai! Pollute our spring once more and I will see you dragging your legs on the ground, unable to walk, because of Chowilau's power of *tamochpolo*! Four times I say it. . . . Listen, so you may know the truth when you hear it!"

No one answered him. The old Navajo sat face down. The children clung to their mothers with frightened faces. The angry young man bit his lip as he scowled.

It was enough. John rose and we stood up with him.

"I do not know what we are to do," said the old Navajo with dignity.

"Keep your sheep away from our sacred shrine," answered John. "But come see me when you are in Oraibi. We will have coffee perhaps." With this last rebuke he walked out.

This immemorially had been the Hopi way of protecting their ancient rights. Their ruins and sacred shrines, their rock writing, and their religious faith—these were the titles to their land that no secular power could refute.

8. THE PROFESSOR AND THE PROPHET

It was a difficult winter for the two Bears and me. The kachina night dances were being held in the kivas of every village, and indomitably we went to every one. Gorgeous as they were, each was an ordeal. They began about midnight and lasted until almost dawn. Huddling outside in the dark for an hour until we were admitted into the kiva, we almost froze in the bitter cold. Once inside, crowded against the wall in a mass of Hopis, we sweated without escape. All of us came down with colds and hollow coughs that could not be cured with the simple remedies at hand.

The dust stirred up by the kachinas, vigorously dancing hour after hour in the stuffy kiva, was worse. All three of us, as well as the Hopis, suffered from inflamed eyelids. A particularly aggravating infection settled in my right eye. Every evening after supper I would lie on the couch and Brown Bear, on her knees on the floor, would patiently open the little pocket of pus with a needle.

Irritable from our enforced intimacy, we wanted to get away. But bad weather still confined us to New Oraibi. All day a heavy mist hung over the mesas, freezing a thin coat of ice on the road that made driving too dangerous. One morning the mist lifted, and with it our spirits. White Bear and I went on a long hike to the shrine of Aponivi, the westernmost and highest spur of Third Mesa. We came back late that afternoon, tired and grimy, only to find that the hot-water heater had burst and none of us could take a bath until a new one could be sent from Flagstaff a week later. Such annoying discomforts only accentuated the differences of opinion between us.

How small but aggravating they were!

Brown Bear persisted in typing all references to the mythical personage known as Kokyangwuti, or Spider Woman, as Spider *Lady*—because, as she said, a lady was more dignified.

"I simply can't have your editing these Hopi myths in accordance with rules of modern etiquette," I told her crossly. "If I can't have the material literally as it was given, I don't want it!"

A few mornings later White Bear blew up when I questioned his description of a male-and-female *paho*. This was a complex and exquisitely made prayer-feather consisting of two willow sticks mounted against a turkey feather, to which was tied a small corn-husk sack containing a pinch of corn pollen and a drop of honey, a downy eagle feather, and two small twigs. Intricately symbolic as it was, our accuracy of description and interpretation was mandatory. Hence I disputed White Bear's insistence that the willow stick with a facet cut in the upper end signified the male stick. "That is the female stick, White Bear. Look here!" I opened before him a copy of the journal of the pioneer ethnologist Alexander M. Stephen containing a drawing of the *paho*.

I might have waved a red flag in front of a bull. White Bear jumped up, bellowing with rage. "I know you now! You go by these ethnologists who have lied about my people! You won't accept my word as the spokesman for my people. You got to print just what I say or I'll quit!"

For answer I laid before him a page of manuscript dictated by his father which described the *paho* just as Stephen had drawn it. "Either your father is wrong or you are," I told him sternly. "Now you go back to him and find out who has been trying to give me false information. And don't come back till you can bring me one of those *pahos* itself!"

Late that afternoon White Bear, affable as ever, returned with a *paho* and a drawing of it correctly labelled.

Time and again such little quarrels were patched up only to break out again. But that spring our troubles came to a head.

The weather cleared and I left for a brief trip to Los Angeles for some supplementary research. The morning after I arrived I received a telephone call from the Angel of Wall Street saying that White Bear had quit the project without warning; Dodagee the Dictator was pushing him too hard. Despite the fact that we were far behind and White Bear's abrupt abandonment of the project placed the Foundation in an embarrassing position, I felt a little sorry for White Bear. I suspected that his inner tensions had suffered pressures from another source too; this was confirmed when I returned to finish up the project alone.

Brown Bear was threatening a marital rupture. She planned to go off alone, whispering darkly that she might not come back. This lonely Reservation, over which seemed to hang a miasma of defeat and decay, was an unhealthy place for her to live. But what would happen to White Bear without her combative spirit and acute sense of material reality? Their situation epitomized the whole relationship between their respective races. This was now pointed up by a significant incident.

That April morning about nine-thirty Chief Tawakwaptiwa died at the age of 106. John Lansa and his wife Mina, with whom he had been living in Oraibi and who had touched his body, conducted the purification ceremony. It was very simple. They burned juniper branches and pitch from a piñon on a stone in the middle of the floor. Facing the smouldering fire, they put one foot at a time in the smoke, letting it rise through the legs and body to the head. Each of them then gathered a handful of ashes and earth, waved it in four circles above their heads, and returned it to the fire. The old man's body was now dressed in one of his ceremonial costumes—that of the Eototo Kachina, and wrapped in a blanket. John then carried it to a cranny in the cliffs west of the village, and sealed it in with stones and boulders. The whole procedure was accomplished within an hour after his death.

The obstreperous old chief had never been liked by either

Hopis or whites and there were few who mourned him. His passing, however, raised a new flood of conjectures about his successor. Papa Bear was not named. He was too old, a Christian, and not willing to leave New Oraibi. There were two other brothers, but they were not named either. Was it possible, I wondered, that the choice would fall upon White Bear?

The prospect aroused some uneasy visions in me. I could see White Bear, clothed in the mantle of his idealistic dreams, discarding all vestiges of his Christian and school training, even his golf clubs, and moving back to the ruin of Old Oraibi on its high mesatop. The Village Chief of scarcely a hundred impoverished people waiting for the cataclysmic destruction of the white world that would leave him untouched to restore this ancient Camelot as the citadel of a new and resplendent Hopi world.

Yet I could not envision Brown Bear quite so clearly as Mrs. Chief, abandoning her threatened trip and enduring up there in loneliness and squalor until this ancient prophecy came true. Nor could I see my own role sharply delineated. White Bear months before had given me a Hopi name from his own Coyote Clan— Kukutema, Always Looking Ahead, assuring me that I would be reborn a Hopi in the new Fifth World. It was a high compliment and I had accepted clanship with him in full sincerity, for I had developed an affection for him in spite of our frequent differences. But now, full of forebodings and troubled by warning dreams, my rational nature and irascible humor asserted themselves. If White Bear were named Chief, would he revoke my Hopi citizenship in the coming new world and condemn me to destruction? Or would he resume work on our project and create for me the post of Foreign Minister or Secretary Without Portfolio? But what about Old Dan and Mister Hopi? Would they and the official spokesmen for all the other Hopi villages tamely submit to the leadership of this shy and retiring man who had never participated in their ceremonies?

These profane conjectures revealed, of course, a fault in my own conception of Hopi character. More and more I had felt the soundness of the intuitional depth and scope of Hopi ceremonialism as contrasted to the superficiality of our own rational materialism. Yet the better I knew the Hopis, the more signs I detected of their obsession with the mythological past that alienated them from all other peoples and modern life. How could they believe in the wholeness of Creation, the brotherhood of all sentient beings, yet stand so aloof? How could I myself subscribe to the validity of their religious belief and at the same time view them as abnormal because they adhered to it? These questions were not simple. I began to feel that they involved not only our conceptions of nature, but of time.

But White Bear was not named Village Chief of Oraibi; no one was named. Old Oraibi remained a leaderless, archaeological ruin, the steeple of its lightning-struck Mennonite mission church sticking up into the lurid sunset like a scorched thumb.

Obviously we all had come to an impasse, and I too needed to get away for a better perspective. So we parted: Brown Bear returning East, and I to my own home in New Mexico, leaving White Bear to his own resources in New Oraibi. Would we ever return? I wondered.

How wonderful it was to leave those parched mesas; to return to my own small ranch in the high, forested mountains; to Indian friends of nearly thirty years. My ranch adjoined their Reservation and they frequently rode horseback from the pueblo to visit or to help with the chores. The mere sight of them, wrapped in their blankets and with their long hair braids, threw the Hopis into better perspective. All these Taos Indians had Spanish names by which they were generally known and it was rare for one to use his Tiwa name outside the pueblo. Nor did I ever know one, outside of the officers duly appointed by the Council, who proclaimed himself a spokesman for the rest. Well adjusted to modern life, they mixed freely with their Spanish and Anglo neighbors while maintaining the dignity of their own beliefs and customs.

Other visitors came too. The State Department's cultural exchange bureau included Taos on the itinerary of foreign visitors to America. On hurried trips from Washington and New York to San Francisco and Los Angeles, they always stopped over to see the classic, twin pyramids of Taos Pueblo. Whether they came from Europe, Asia, or Africa, their questions were always the same:

What is the status of your remaining Indians now? Do they still resent having been almost exterminated or do they now feel part of your social fabric? Do they still maintain their own beliefs and customs, or are they culturally adapting to modern life? What do the rest of the people of your country feel about Indians now?

What they all were really asking was simple: What will be the future of primitive peoples throughout the world now that the era of colonialization is over?

Once more I felt that the answer to such a weighty question must include the mysterious factor of time—a time with a context far different from our usual conception of it.

Meanwhile the three-sided difference between the two Bears and myself was being resolved by enterprising and aggressive Brown Bear who had gone to New York to patch up White Bear's break with the Angel of Wall Street. Shortly there came a note that she had returned to New Oraibi and bought a house. This was followed by some new material from White Bear, indicating that he had resumed work on the project. In July, I too returned to work. This time I took the Professor and my wife Rose for a brief visit.

The Professor was an old, dear friend of many years. Into his slender, nervous little body, as into an encyclopedia, he had packed an amazing compendium of knowledge. From its neat compartments he could draw forth instantly anything you wanted to know about literature and science, Greek syntax, Etruscan art, and the subtleties of Chinese philosophy. His eyes twinkled behind his glasses and he had a quick laugh. He was a gentleman of manners and a jolly companion.

That winter he had wanted very much to come for a kachina dance. "Let me know the night it will be," he wrote. "I shall arrive by plane at Flagstaff at 4:05 that afternoon. You can pick me up there. Allowing an hour and a half for the drive to New Oraibi, we will have two hours for dinner and a chat before the dance. After the dance is over, say about 3:00 in the morning, we can drive back to Flagstaff where I catch my plane out at 5:15. Does this schedule sound reasonable to you?"

I wrote back an emphatic NO. It was the dead of winter. A heavy snow might occur that would make the 125-mile drive difficult or impossible. Furthermore, kachina dances were not scheduled at a precise time on a certain night. One might not be held until the night after he arrived, and might not begin until after midnight. On top of this, we might have to stand outside for an hour before the kiva was opened to us. "So be sure, Professor," I cautioned him, "to bring your pills."

That did it. The Professor had an insane dread of catching cold.

We arrived just a few days before the Niman Kachina ceremony. The Professor was bubbling with good spirits, his alert mind ready to rationalize all new impressions. The comfortable four-room house Brown Bear had bought was not far from the trading post, and White Bear had worked hard to fix it up. Generous and hospitable as always, they made up a bed in the living room for Rose and prepared the back room—Pneumonia's Boudoir—in my little house below Pumpkin Seed Point for the Professor.

Brown Bear spared no effort to set the table with her best cooking. How she loved company! She even took a drink with us out of the bottle Rose had brought. I was a little leery about that bottle of whiskey standing so brazenly on the kitchen table, for few Hopis drank and White Bear himself viewed liquor as a prime white evil. So now, while the four of us grew merry in the kitchen, I kept a wary eye on our host. White Bear sulked by himself in the living room, distinctly displeased. But at dinner time he sat down at the table with us. I was proud of his forebearance.

What a strange pair they made, these two men sitting at the table, the Professor and the Prophet. For it was natural that White Bear, when skillfully drawn out by the Professor, assumed his role of Prophet. His indictment of the white race for its injustices to the red race was magnificent. More eloquent still was his prophecy of how the continent would be destroyed by a great cataclysm as retribution for the violation of the Creator's life pattern. Only the Hopi Reservation would be saved in order that the Hopis could reestablish their ancient order.

"How do you know so certainly that this will take place, White Bear?" the Professor asked gently.

"It is the prophecy!" White Bear's voice shook with emotion. "It is written on our sacred tablets. It is written in the rock writing found throughout our land. It is written in our hearts. We Hopis know!"

It was quite possible that the Professor, even with his wide experience, had never encountered before such a mythological context manifested as a living form of faith. His extreme rationality had no answer. He sat quietly spellbound, without argument. I was proud of his forebearance. What a good time we were going to have!

It indeed started out auspiciously. The two Bears were delighted to show off the Reservation to Rose and the Professor. We drove to Old Oraibi to prowl through its ruins, to Hotevilla and Bakavi. We climbed to the top of First Mesa to see its three villages: Hano, Sichomovi, and spectacular Walpi. The Home Dance of the Niman Kachina ceremony at Shongopovi on Second Mesa was magnificent as always. Next day, fortunately, there was another kachina dance in the little village of Shipaulovi. Rose and Brown Bear giggled and gossipped; the Professor and White Bear talked of New York and Philadelphia.

"A charming fellow!" asserted the Professor, hugging me with exuberance. "How glad I am I came. What a capital vacation!"

What happened then, and just when, I didn't know. But White Bear suddenly closed up like a clam. His only answers to the Professor's questions were curt replies. He sulked in the living room alone, ate his meals in silent preoccupation, and went out to sit on the porch in darkness. We were all embarrassed.

The Professor, a sensitive man, was worried. "I have offended him in some way. If I could find out how, I would like to apologize."

"I'm sure you haven't said anything," said Brown Bear. "He's just moody. It'll wear off. Don't worry about it."

There was only one day more remaining of the Professor's visit. To celebrate it we decided to drive to the ruined village of prehistoric Sikyatki and collect potsherds. Rose and Brown Bear enthusiastically made sandwiches and off we went. White Bear's somber mood, however, had not changed. He drove silently, his placid face set stiffly as concrete.

"You know where the ruin is, don't you?" the Professor asked him pleasantly, to make conversation.

"Why shouldn't I?" snapped White Bear. "Sikyatki was the

home of my own Coyote Clan!"

The ruin lay about three miles northeast of First Mesa. We drove as far as we could on a sandy desert road, then left the car and began walking over the dunes and the ridges of bare, jagged rock. The July day was extremely hot; and the sun, beating down on the fine white sand, reflected back into our bent, perspiring faces. Walking became difficult. Yet White Bear, far ahead, kept beckoning with impatience and pointing to the ruin ahead. It was always just ahead; when we got there, it lay still farther ahead. At last, confronting the high escarpment of the mesa, we could go no farther. The ruin was nowhere in sight.

"I'd think you'd know where Sikyatki is if it was the home of your own clan!" said Brown Bear petulantly.

White Bear was embarrassed; he was hopelessly lost.

"Let's forget Sikyatki, Bear, and drive to the ruins of Awatovi instead," I suggested. "The Professor would love to see the famous ruins."

"I would indeed," replied the Professor tactfully.

White Bear whirled to face the Professor, his face livid with anger. "You people have set foot in Awatovi for the last time! You know what you did!"

Instantly, in a flash of intuition, I knew what had brought on White Bear's bitter mood of the last two days. Before I could say anything, White Bear flung around and strode off rapidly toward a far ridge to the east. It was impossible for the rest of us to follow him. We slowly trudged back to the car, climbed inside to escape the blinding heat, and began uncorking our water bottles.

Almost an hour passed before a horseman rode up: a Hopi policeman. He had happened to meet White Bear and showed him the location of Sikyatki. He had then ridden to us to point out the way. We started the car and drove to the bottom of the rocky foothill to which he had directed us. Up on top we could see White Bear scratching for potsherds.

The Professor apparently had forgotten White Bear's strange outburst of anger. He seemed also to have forgotten that he had suffered, not too long ago, a coronary attack. Flushed with enthusiastic discovery, he began scrambling up the steep slope with the agility of a goat. The two women and myself panted behind.

Sikyatki lay on the ridge below an outcrop of dark jagged rock. Below it a few ancient peach trees protruded from dunes of yellow sand. Scarcely anything of the ruin was visible. Drifting sand covered the fallen walls. The great plaza was overgrown with weeds. Yet the whole desolate waste was still littered with broken pottery—perhaps the most distinctive pottery ever found north of Mexico.

"Look!" cried Rose, excited as a child, holding up a great shard on which showed the stylistic head of a bird.

"Yes, but see what I found!" yelled the Professor, holding up another.

Poking in the sand, digging out handsful of exquisite fragments to bulge our pockets and fill our empty sandwich bags, we spent an exhilarating afternoon and came home to Brown Bear's farewell dinner. It was dusk when we finished and went out on the porch to sit. White Bear, however, did not join us; he was still grumpy. When Brown Bear and Rose went in to do the dishes, the Professor asked me suddenly, "What did White Bear mean this afternoon when he blew up at me? I still can't imagine how I offended him!"

"You didn't. It was my fault. I must have mentioned to him sometime that you were a Catholic."

The Professor looked perplexed.

"Listen," I said. "I want to tell you the story of Awatovi."

When the first Spanish conquerors arrived in the New World, Awatovi was one of the most important Hopi villages, reported to have a population of 800 people. Missionary efforts to convert the Hopis to Christianity began with the establishment of missions at Awatovi, Oraibi, and Shongopovi, and *visitas* at Walpi and Mishongnovi. Conversion followed the customary pattern of Spanish conquest. The Hopis were enslaved to build the churches and supply the needs of the priests; they were publicly whipped and killed when caught in acts of idolatry. By 1680 the Indians could stand no more. In a concerted revolt against the "Slave Church," all the pueblos throughout the Southwest rose against their masters. The Indians killed nearly 500 Spaniards, tore down the churches, sacked Santa Fe, and drove the survivors back to Mexico.

Twelve years later the Spaniards returned, offering forgiveness and gifts of sheep and horses to all pueblos that would resubmit to Spanish rule. Seventy-three pueblos accepted these peaceful terms. Today they are known by the names of Christian saints given them, and the people's common language is Spanish — the Christian-Spanish patina under which they have been able to preserve their own pattern of life.

The Hopi villages were the notable exception. They stubbornly rejected all inroads of Spanish culture and Christianity. Then burst the terrible calamity. In 1700 a Spanish priest visited Awatovi and persuaded seventy-three Hopis to be baptized. With this effort to reestablish Christianity, the hatred of the Hopis for the Slave Church burst into flame. At a secret meeting the chiefs of the other villages decided to destroy Awatovi for its betrayal. On the designated night the attack was made. The inflamed Hopis swarmed through the streets murdering men, women, and children, and setting fire to the village. Still their fury was not spent. The following day they returned to smoking Awatovi, tore down house walls, destroyed every household article used by the massacred inhabitants, and dragged the survivors off to torture. By nightfall the destruction of Awatovi was complete. It was an empty, smoking ruin abandoned to the elements and left to be buried by drifting sand. The ethnologist, J. W. Fewkes, who excavated it in 1892, reported finding such evidences of wholesale slaughter that he was deterred from further work by the response of his horror-struck Hopi workmen.

This complete obliteration of Awatovi rooted out forever the dominance of the foreign Christian Slave Church. Still today, more than two and a half centuries later, there is no Catholic church in the villages of Second and Third Mesa although the Hopis have permitted the entrance of other denominational mission churches; and their resentment against whites is focused upon the Christian Catholic. When John F. Kennedy was elected the first Catholic President of the United States, the Hopis in New Oraibi cast only one vote for him against sixty votes for Nixon.

The Professor listened to this horrible, tragic story of Awatovi without comment, staring out into the velvety darkness. In a little while Brown Bear and Rose came out on the porch. "Where's White Bear?" he asked quietly.

"Oh, he's in the kitchen trying to fix the rubber insulation on that old refrigerator door," answered Brown Bear.

"I'm a good hand at that sort of thing. Maybe I can help." He went inside. An hour later he was still there, down on his knees, sleeves rolled up, working with pliers and screwdriver. White Bear's face glowed like a full Hopi moon. His mood had passed. He was cheerful and friendly, and even proposed that they share a melon as a reward for their work.

How can one measure today the cumulative effects of the tragedy of Awatovi? The Hopis' complete destruction of one of their largest villages, the fratricidal mass murder of their own people for displaying tolerance toward a new faith, betrayed their own tradition as a People of Peace dedicated to helping maintain in unbroken harmony the lives of every entity, plant, animal, and man. Yet if its guilt is stamped upon the heart of every Hopi, we too must bear the same searing guilt for our failure to give them a new, living faith. It is no paradox that the continued drive by missionaries of many creeds and sects has resulted in the conversion of more and more Indians everywhere. Their choice has been not between their ancient beliefs and the tenets of Christianity which we preach on Sunday and ignore in practice the rest of the week. They have found it merely expedient to wear a Christian mask for practical, secular purposes, while still preserving their mythological faith in the forces of life itself.

Awatovi is a seed that will continue to grow until, watered by our mutual tears of forgiveness, it will blossom into the spirit of our accomplished brotherhood. If it reflects, as I believe it does, an imperishable Hopi memory of what may seem to us an almost forgotten incident of the vanished historical past, it also reveals the context of a time with dimensions far different than our own.

9. TIME

That the Indian concept of time is far different from our own is a truism asserted by every perceptive observer. Just what this difference is, none of them adequately explains. Nor is it fully illustrated by the *koshare* or Pueblo Indian clown I once saw dancing into a tourist-crowded plaza, pointing derisively to an alarm clock strapped on his arm and shouting, "Time to be hungry!" I cannot quite explain it myself, for time is a great abstraction that cannot be expressed in rational terms. Yet sometimes I awake in the silence of the night with an intuitive feeling of its mysterious context. It is as if I am no longer caught in a moving flow, but becalmed in a placid sea that has depth and content, a life and meaning all its own. At these moments of utter peace I feel absolved from the necessity of hurrying through space to reach a point in time; or, yes, of becoming hungry at the stroke of a clock. For time seems then a living, organic element that mysteriously helps to fashion our own shape and growth.

It is the same feeling engendered by the great ruins of ancient America—the ceremonial complexes of pyramid and observatory, temple and tomb, still compelling our wonder in the jungles of Yucatan, in the Valley of Mexico at San Juan Teotihuacan, and on the summit of Monte Alban in Oaxaca. Here, 1,500 years before Christ, 3,000 years before this continent was known to Europe, the Indians of Mexico erected the first observatory in the New World and evolved the calendar which became the basis of their religion. The deeper meaning of these great stone edifices is unknown to us, so foreign are their shapes and proportions, the very inclination of their planes—the terms by which they exalted the journey of the spirit out of matter, and equated the invisible dimensions of time and space with eternity.

Nowhere is this more apparent than in the Toltecan sacred city of Teotihuacan, The Place Where Men Became Gods, some thirty miles outside Mexico City. Dating from the first century B.C. and not yet wholly excavated, this sacred city was the oldest and largest metropolis in Mesoamerica—fifty-five square miles in area. The heart of this immense and majestic ruin, completely paved and covering seven square miles, was divided into two sections. The lower section comprised a vast quadrangle composed in horizontal lines of masonry. Within it was set the Temple of Quetzalcoatl, its sides decorated with 365 heads of the Plumed Serpent carved in high relief, one for each day of the year. The name derived from two Nahual words: *quetzal,* a bird of resplendent plumage, and *coatl,* a snake, signifying the union of heaven and earth, of matter and spirit. Quetzalcoatl, then, was a god of self-sacrifice and penitence who redeemed man through the conflict of opposites; the supreme diety, the Redeemer.

The upper section to the east, toward the rising sun, was architectured with vertical lines and dedicated to Heaven, counterpointing the lower, horizontally laid-out section dedicated to Earth. It was dominated by two great pyramids, one each for the sun and the moon. The Pyramid of the Sun was immense, rising 210 feet high from a square base whose sides each measured 726 feet. Its east-west axis deviated seventeen degrees north from the true line in order to orient the pyramid to the spot at that latitude where the sun fell below the horizon on the day of its passage through the sky's zenith.

Linking the two sections was a noble avenue, one and a quarter miles long and forty-four yards wide, called Miccaotli, the Street of the Dead. It led past terraced buildings in which religious neophytes probably underwent ceremonies signifying their ritual death to the world of matter before they ascended the Pyramid of the Sun to attain the luminous consciousness of spirit. This was the ritual path taken by Quetzalcoatl before he was transformed into the planet Venus. It is the same path still followed by Venus, which first appears in the western sky, disappears below the horizon for several days, and then reappears in the eastern sky to reunite with the sun.

Hence the Pyramid of the Sun, as Laurette Sejourne points out, was dedicated to the Fifth Sun or Fifth World in which man, synthesizing all the elements of his past, must now by a reconciliation of opposites make his final ascent out of matter into spirit. All the great stone monuments along the longitudinal axis of the sacred city were oriented in terms of it. Teotihuacan was thus astronomically laid out with geometric precision in the shape of a vast stone mandala, a quincunx with four cardinal points and a synthesizing center symbolizing the sun, the light of consciousness within man himself.

How little we know about these vast ruins, so many of which are still covered by the rubble and drifted sand of a thousand years. And still less of the meaning that once imbued them with life, that gave birth to a great civilization on a continent unknown to the savage tribes roaming the forests of Europe. We can only stand appalled before this conception in stone of universal wholeness, of cosmic balance, which expresses above all the mystery of a space-time continuum alien to our own preoccupation with a linear, flowing time.

Perhaps more than any other people these Toltecs and Zapotecs, Aztecs and Mayas were obsessed with the flux of time, with the relationship of every individual to it as an element in their own natures. Still today all Indian America lives in the element of time as livingly real as the elements of fire, air, water, and earth.

We Euro-Americans must question our own concept of time as a medium of linear measurement. The lives of a star and a stone are measured by millenia; the evanescent life of a moth is measured in hours. Yet nothing on our scale indicates that vertical dimension of time in which the life-cycle of each is completed in accord with its own unique design of being.

To us time is a shallow, horizontal stream flowing out from the past, through the present, into the future. We are increasingly obsessed with the sense of its constant movement as it increasingly loses all relation to astronomical time. The clock ticks ever faster. Every tick converts a segment of the distant future into the present, yet this present is swept so swiftly into the past that we have no present left to experience in its fullness.

This conception of time as a flowing horizontal stream, an unwinding scroll or ribbon, accounts for our fascination with histories and biographies. They enable us to watch the scroll unwind. What we see marked on it, nevertheless, are largely the spatial locations and astronomical dates fixing man's entrance into the stream and his exit from it, with the jutting landmarks observed during his linear journey. The history of a nation or an individual, it seems to me, consists of far more than these events that protrude above the surface like the visible tips of submerged icebergs. Deep below lie the invisible forces in which they have their true being. All the great movements of history—the Crusades, revolutions, and the present world unrest—are impelled by the laws of some inner necessity as instinctive, inexplicable, and certain as those that dictate the migration of swallows to San Juan Capistrano. The historical events are empty cocoons discarded by the spirit that moved through them.

We are no less obsessed with the portion of the unrolling ribbon we call the future. We keep dividing it into ever smaller segments, marking each with an entry. Perhaps no other people have been so infernally preoccupied with programs, schedules, budgets. "I have no time!" This is the despairing cry of twentieth-century man, panicky with unrest, as he rushes ever faster from the past to the future over the knife-edge of the unlived present.

Fortunately there are a few who are beginning to have uneasy qualms about our "objective" view of time. Could it be possible that time is subjective, existing only in the mind? For behind us stretch geologic eras of ever-lengthening time-spans into the immeasurable archeozoic which as it recedes merges into azoic time, and it into cosmic time that curves back into the psychozoic time to come. The magic circle in which the past links with the future, without beginning or end. The immemorial snake of the ancients, swallowing its own tail.

Indian time—what is it, really, abstract as it seems?

Benjamin Lee Whorf in his profound analysis of the Hopi language calls it a "timeless language." It has no three-tense system like our own. It contains no imaginary plurals like a period of ten days; a Hopi attending a ten-day ceremony says simply that he stayed until the tenth day. His time always has zero dimensions; it cannot be given a number greater than one. The Hopi language thus avoids the artificiality of expressing time by linear relation, as units in a row. Our "length of time" is expressed by the Hopi not as a linear measurement, but as a relationship between two events. These events reflect the intensity of the observer, for time varies with each observer. Hopi time, then, is a true psychological time, Whorf insists. "For if we inspect consciousness we find no past, present, future; everything is in consciousness, and everything in consciousness *is*, and is together." Hence the Hopis' time is not a motion. It is a duration, a storing up of change, of power that holds over into later events. Everything that ever happened, still is— though in a different form. A constant anticipation and preparation that becomes realization. A sense of ever becoming within a duration of immovable time.

This supreme time which has no beginning or end, no stages

or breaks, and which is motionless and boundless, is also known as Duration or *Parakála* in the religious philosophy of the East, Shakta Vedantism. It has two aspects. It may be statically condensed into a point (now) which is the pivotal center of every event. And it may expand dynamically into a boundless continuum (always) which is the experience of Duration involving past, present, and future.

Space, like time, has the same twofold aspect, shrinking to a center (here) and swelling in a boundless continuum (everywhere), the evolution and involution being the pulse of life itself. Nor do the Hopis have our concept of static three-dimensional space. The distance between events includes time—not as a linear measurement, but as a temporal relation between them. For the realm of objective events stretches away to the realm of mythical events which can only be known subjectively. Hence the immediacy and emotional strength of mythical happenings as enacted in Hopi ceremonialism. May we question whether time and space comprise one single continuum? And may it be equated with what we call the all-embracing Self?

In this conception of time lies the secret of the power and validity of Hopi ceremonialism. There are nine great ceremonies in the annual cycle: three in the winter, three in the summer, and three in the fall.

The first group portrays in a profound three-act drama the three phases in the dawn of Creation. In Wuwuchim all forms of life are germinated—plant, animal, and man; and the creative fire with which life begins is lighted. Soyal, the second phase, lays out the pattern for life's development. The wide and naked earth is solidified; the sun is turned back on the night of the winter solstice to give warmth and strength to budding life; and the kachinas arrive from their other-world homes to consecrate its growth. Powamu, which follows it, purifies the life-pattern laid out by Soyal. During it the life germinated by Wuwuchim makes its first appearance in physical form, and mankind as children are initiated by the kachinas into its spiritual meaning.

The second group of ceremonies—Niman Kachina, the Snake-Antelope, and Flute ceremonies—is held during the period of the summer solstice. Time has not moved. But within its immovable duration, the anticipation and preparation embodied in the winter ceremonies now become realization. Their stored up power transforms potential events into manifest form—into the full development of all life forms, the summer rains, the growth, maturity, and fruition of crops. With this, the host of kachinas have done their work and return again to their other-world homes.

The third group of ceremonies follows in the fall, concluding with the harvest. They are ritually concerned with the harvesting not only of the crops but of the prayers planted during the winter. Lakon, Maraw, and Owaqlt are women's ceremonies and hence they have another meaning. For now the earth is hardening again, the days are growing shorter. It is time to make ready for germination of life anew. Hence the accent on sexual symbols, woman being the receptacle and carrier for the seed of mankind which will link the concluding cycle with the new one to begin.

There is no mistaking the meaning of these nine intricate and interlocked ceremonies. They form a web of relationships that includes not only man but the sub-orders of the plant and animal kingdoms, the super-orders of spiritual beings, the kachinas, and the living entities of the earth and planetary bodies above. Interrelated in an ecological pattern of correlative obligations, they dramatize a creative plan whose power supersedes that of the limited human will. A plan that has no beginning and no end in time. For Creation did not take place, once and for all, at a certain time—

at precisely nine o'clock on a morning in 4004 B.C. as Archbishop Usher once maintained. The creative plan is repeated endlessly outside and within man himself.

These ceremonies, we must observe, do not constitute a formal Sunday religion of moral tenets exhorted by priest and preacher for the benefit of the laity. The Hopis have no priests, no consecrated or professional intermediaries. Each Hopi man participates in his turn in one or more of the ceremonies; and each ceremony lasts from nine to twenty days. Nor is the observance of Hopi religion restricted to them. All Hopis are abjured to pray, to hold good thoughts. For thought is power; it is the seed planted to bear fruition in durational time, the anticipation that becomes realization.

All history, as well, is embodied in the ever-living present. I have been repeatedly annoyed and perplexed at the Hopis' complete disregard of dates and chronological sequences. They have related incidents which apparently occurred during their own memory but which, as I found out later, actually happened a century or more ago. The importance of such events is not measured by their relative significance in historical time, but by the emotional intensity they created—as the hatred of the white Slave Church which impelled the destruction of Awatovi. Hopis at Oraibi still persistently point out great ruts scraped into the rocky mesa top by the ends of huge logs. These logs, it will be explained, they had been forced to drag from the mountains nearly a hundred miles away for use as roof beams in the mission church. A casual visitor, looking vainly for the church, may learn with surprise that the ruts were made three centuries ago.

The European conquest of all Indian America illustrates this on a continental scale. Seldom has one race been so completely subjugated by another for so long. Yet after four and a half centuries, white domination is still a surface veneer. A story once told me in Mexico City by Anita Brenner is not unusual. A little village church in the remote mountains of Michoacan was noted for years for the devout attention it received. From miles around, Indians trudged in over the steep trails to kneel at its altar and bank it with flowers. Even the simple young rural priest in charge was baffled at this mysterious devotion on the part of such usually ignorant and obstinate Indians. . . . Until a slight earthquake overturned the altar, revealing a squat stone Aztec idol underneath. The story happens to be true, but it could well be an apt parable in which the altar signifies a religion made rationally conscious, under which lies the mythological content of the unconscious, that one great pool of life and time.

I first became aware of this subterranean quality of land and people many years ago when alone on horseback I rode down the length of Mexico. Small clusters of adobes or *jacales* were the only villages in these remote sierras. A man plowing a small corn *milpa* with the crotch of a tree. A barefoot woman grinding the kernels on a concave stone, the Aztec *metatl* now called the *metate*. Patting the dough into *tortillas,* the Aztec *tlaxcalli,* and cooking them on a griddle, the *comal* or *comalli.* A group of naked children leading my horse to their mother's hut. Here I asked permission to sleep on the floor with the family, rolled in my own *serape.* Then I waited a day or two until someone could accompany me to the next village.

A guide was necessary, for in this unmarked wilderness there were no roads and only an Indian could follow the dim trails trod by the bare feet of his father's fathers. I always tried to obtain for the day's journey a young boy or an old man; not only because they could be better spared from the fields, but because they talked more freely. With them trudging beside my mule, the land and people took on meaning. My guides unveiled the hidden names and spiritual meanings of physical landmarks, the peak, the gorge, the secret spring; and they explained the medicinal use of unknown herbs. It was not unusual to encounter an isolated shrine in which had been placed small clay idols like those planted in the corn fields. I remember my surprise at seeing one young boy gathering flowers and carrying them to deposit on top of a small hill. When I asked him why, he simply scraped off the rubble of sand and pebbles from its sides to reveal the pyramidal outline of cut stones.

It was an old charcoal burner who finally summarized the meaning of my journey of three months and a thousand miles. He had guided me to the top of an abysmal gorge in the mountains to show me the trail leading down to the village below. It was late afternoon and the tenuous mountain mist was lifting. In a moment it all spread out with the incomparable beauty of an immense intaglio. The great mountain walls still shrouded with mist. The tiny valley below. And in it the ancient village—a great, empty cathedral of blackened stone mounted in a central plaza and surrounded by adobe houses, huts, and corrals. A village, he explained, whose people still spoke Aztec.

"How beautiful! A man could live here forever!" I exclaimed in a burst of extravagant praise.

The old Indian turned to me an impassive face still blackened with charcoal. Neither his eyes nor his voice betrayed an ironic amusement. *"Pues.* How long are *you* staying?"

That is the story of the Spanish conquest. Of a race of foreign invaders who built their cathedrals in these tiny villages, imposed their tongue and customs on the people, and spread their veneer of conquest over all the land, but never reached its roots. The cake is still iced with baroque and mosaic decorations, still bejewelled with the great cities they founded. But the land and the people remain unchanged. The pulse of life is not echoed by the church bell and the factory whistle. It is still the pat-pat-pat of earth-brown hands shaping a *tortilla* from Indian maize shaped by the earth itself.

The Mexican revolution against Spain was not the result of Napoleon's crossing the Pyrenees. Nor can the new tremors of unrest now shaking the Sierra Madres and the Andes be attributed to political and economic stresses. These but explain their effects, not their causes. For they are subterranean movements rising from deep within the soul of man and land. The present resurgence of ancient Toltec, Aztec, Maya, and Inca values in modern architecture, art, and music show how deeply they are rooted, and they are but a prelude to the re-emergence of Indian values in all fields. I cannot but believe that the final flowering of civilization throughout the Western Hemisphere is yet to come and that it will reflect its own indigenous shape and meaning. Like the greatest mountain and smallest insect, it is an organic life-pattern planted in that durational time which mysteriously insures its growth within its own cycle.

We who are frantically racing against the flow of horizontal time, engulfed in its flood of external materialism, fear there is not enough time left for humanity to improve before the world's self-destruction by thermonuclear war. Yet becalmed in a motionless moment of silent night, we may take some comfort from the belief in another dimension that gives us all the worlds and time we need. In it we too may find the power to simply *be,* secure in the faith that the past and the future form one organic whole within us.

10. THE EVIL EYE

Early one winter morning while I was still in bed, White Bear burst into the house in a state of visible distress. His usually placid face was drawn and pale. His big brown eyes were pools of anxiety. His hands trembled as he took off his gloves.

"What's the matter?" I cried.

"Somebody has put a spell on me. I'm going to die!"

I looked at him with amazement. It seemed impossible, that early in the morning, to believe his terror of witchcraft. Yet there he stood, frozen into a posture of helpless immobility by the stare of some invisible, evil eye. I jumped out of bed, turned on the gas heater. "Sit down and tell me about it."

It had happened once before in his family. His oldest sister had been killed by witchcraft, and his mother had got Otto Pentiwa to find out who had done it. The details were horrible and pathetic. Now it was his turn.

"You know who did it, then?"

He stood up, irresolute and shaken, then suddenly leaned over me and whispered a name in my ear.

The revelation seemed to switch a light on a number of trivial incidents and human relationships that had perplexed me for months. We sat looking at each other like guilty accomplices to a tragic mystery.

"She has the power. You know now," he said at last.

I backed against the stove to confront him. This was not an empty superstition to be laughed away. It was an intangible reality that demanded the deepest understanding I could summon to meet it.

"I will see this witch. I will tell her of my dreams, of my own power. She will know then that her power is useless. I will break this spell. You are not going to die. Do you believe me?"

He did not answer, but the muscles in has face relaxed, his

111

body became more pliable. Shaking hands formally, he went out the door.

A few evenings later the two Bears and I went over for supper in the big, ramshackle old house in whose tiny apartment they had first lived. It was owned by White Bear's aunt, Elizabeth, who occasionally took in guests; the only place where a meal and a bed might be available to a stranded motorist, a stray tourist, or visiting anthropologist. Their availability depended upon Elizabeth's mood, for she also owned a house in Flagstaff to which she would unpredictably go for a few days or a month. Even when home here, she might not be in a mood to receive a paying guest and would turn him away with no explanation.

Elizabeth was a big-boned, heavy-set woman of resolute character. No one could believe that she was seventy years old. Born a rebel, she preferred her English name of Elizabeth to her Hopi name, Polingaysi. She had been married once, and briefly, to a part-Cherokee. Thereafter she had been a schoolteacher in the Indian Service, being stationed in remote posts, like Chinlee, throughout the Navajo Reservation. She spoke English and Navajo in addition to her native Hopi. Upon her retirement she had moved to New Oraibi where she kept busy every day that she was not in Flagstaff. Her varied interests never exhausted her tremendous vitality. She made pottery, instituted one project after another to promote better education for Hopi children, occasionally made talks in museums as far away as Los Angeles, served as an anthropologist's informant on witchcraft practices, and was currently working on a book with a collaborator—her sad autobiography of a woman neither white nor Hopi. The variety of these activities perplexed me. None of them seemed to engross her full interest—at least for very long. It was as if she were searching for the key to her own many-faceted existence.

Stern, irascible, and resolute, she dominated everyone with whom she came in contact. There was a natural antipathy between her and Brown Bear who too was outspoken and aggressive. This was undoubtedly one of the reasons why Brown Bear had bought a separate house. Elizabeth too I suspected of viewing with disfavor White Bear's obsession with the Hopi past. I myself had known her for several years and liked her.

The ramshackle old house looked warm and inviting as we prepared to enter. But all the rooms were closed up like iceboxes except the kitchen and the adjoining sitting room. Here the oil stove was burning full blast, the lights were lit, and the table already set. Elizabeth was in an excellent mood.

We ate at once, without preliminaries, then gathered around the stove to pop corn. It was mid-January and snow was beginning to fall again. What could be more natural on such a night than to tell ghost stories between handsful of buttered popcorn? Elizabeth, like all Hopis, was an excellent storyteller. Often she turned to White Bear to ask for his version of these familiar tales, but he sat withdrawn and silent.

From ghost stories we turned to dreams, including some of my own. Elizabeth was impressed, particularly by the one in which I had been visited by two ghosts. We began to talk about witchcraft. It was then I began to feel a change in the atmosphere of the room. There was nothing tangible; it simply seemed keyed to a higher vibration, a nervous tension that made me feel curiously apprehensive. Brown Bear began to bristle; one could almost see her hackles rise. Her attitude reflected the indignation and animosity of the whole rational and extroverted white race confronted with an invisible, other-dimensional world which it did not believe existed, but to which, by some curious perversity, it resented being denied admittance. White Bear sat head down, arms wrapped around his

113

body, hands trembling. Elizabeth ignored them both. She faced me; she was dark, stern, and indomitable, with a hard glitter in her eyes.

She was in her element now; and in this realm of the fantastic and inimically unreal, her whole mood had changed. She spoke positively and authoritatively from a conviction rooted deep in her Hopi nature—embodied really in her primeval past. A conviction of the dark, negative aspect of man that lies within us all. What surprised me was the way she seemed to invoke, welcome, and defend it against its counterpart—the light, positive aspect of our dual nature that best expressed itself, among the Hopis, in the profound pattern of their religious belief. She reveled in its betrayal of the human spirit, in the havoc it reaped from doubt, fear, and repression. Too much! Yes, she championed it too vehemently because of her own unconscious fear of it. I suddenly felt I knew Elizabeth.

Of course she wasn't a witch! Yet it was easy to see why White Bear believed she was the one who killed his sister. Shrewd, irascible, and powerful, she jutted out from her docile, gentle neighbors like her own stubborn jaw. And she loved this sense of domination because it hid her own inner trepidation.

"Certainly I believe in ghosts and witches, Elizabeth," I answered lightly. "But I also believe that the invisible powers of the human spirit are stronger. We all have such powers in our fashion. I do myself. Now I'll tell you what I'll do. You bring the most powerful witch here you know and I'll have a duel with her. What do you say?"

As if in answer to this rash and boastful challenge to an incontestable power, the beam of a light flashed full upon us. White Bear jumped up in his corner like a frightened rabbit and stood waiting for the manifestation of a frightening apparition. The light, however, was that of an automobile which had rolled up to the window silently in the falling snow. I flung open the door to see a group of Navajos clambering out of a battered pickup. They came inside, covered with snow and stiff with cold, to stand timidly around the stove. They were too miserable to talk. There were four of them: two young men, an older man, and a woman in evident distress.

"No supper. No bed," Elizabeth said curtly. "The house is closed up."

The sight of hated Navajos restored White Bear's courage. He summoned the effort to dismiss them at once.

The older Navajo man did not protest; but finding his voice, he asked gently if his wife could sit down for a little bit until her strength came back. She looked ill indeed, bent over the stove like a stiff, crooked stick, soaking up warmth with her wan, yellow face and outspread hands. Helped by her husband, she sank down on a chair and stared vacantly across the room.

Gravely he explained their plight. He, his wife, and their two sons lived near Grants, New Mexico, where a doctor in the hospital had examined his wife but had been unable to find anything physically wrong with her. So at four o'clock that morning they all had climbed into their old pickup and started out for New Oraibi. At Gallup, snow had begun to fall. There were no chains for the tires and they had barely made it over the mountain pass near Window Rock. In desolate Steamboat Canyon the road had been blocked; it was necessary to wait two hours until a snowplow came to clear it. Taking turns riding in the open bed of the pickup, crouched down under a blanket, all of them were almost frozen. So all four of them crowded in the front seat. By the time they reached the Crosspoint Trading Post it was dark and the car's headlights kept going out. The post was closed; they were unable to buy coffee and something to eat, or to secure help in fixing

115

the headlights. So they had continued on in dark, cold, and snow, with the headlights constantly flickering out. Now, after a ride of more than 200 miles and sixteen hours, they had arrived at their destination.

"What do you want here?" asked Elizabeth.

"That doctor can't find nothing wrong with my wife. So we bring her here to this medicine man."

"Why didn't you take her to one of your own medicine men?"

"This Hopi. He got the power. That we hear." His two sons nodded assent. Even the sick woman's eyes steadied and brightened.

"What's wrong with her?"

Patiently all three men tried to explain the nature of her curious illness. All day she felt all right, good maybe. Then when the sun went down it happened. It started taking away her life. Her throat tightened like somebody was choking her until she could not swallow and could hardly breathe. This made her chest and belly hurt too. So all night they kept vigil with her, listening to her gasping breaths, until daylight brought relief. "Look, it is night. You see the truth of our words."

It was all too evident in the woman's labored breathing.

"Make her a cup of tea, Elizabeth," I suggested. "She's half-frozen and hasn't had a drink of water since noon."

"I said my house is closed to guests! I'm not serving meals to anybody!"

"Oh come, Elizabeth!" I protested. "You can do that much for this poor woman, even if she is a Navajo. I'll make it myself, with your permission."

Brown Bear stalked into the kitchen, boiled water, and came back with a cup of tea. At sight of it the three men broke into a torrent of protesting Navajo.

"They don't want her to have it!" translated Elizabeth. "Didn't they just get through explaining that she can't swallow after sunset? It ought to be clear to you that a witch has put a spell on her!"

"You tell them that this will break the spell until the medicine man can remove it. Tell them Elizabeth!"

Here it was, hidden like all great mysteries behind an apparently trivial human incident: the strange feud over witchcraft Elizabeth and I had been having all evening, culminating in my somewhat humorous challenge to duel with any witch. There was no doubt that the invisible witch had arrived, manifesting her evil power in the victim before us. Elizabeth seemed to know it too. She stood there irresolute, the focus of a curious tableau: Brown Bear still holding the cup of tea before the gasping woman slumped in her chair, flanked by the Navajos excitedly jabbering in their own language, and White Bear nervously twisting his porkpie hat in his hands. What made her hesitate? The fear of losing face before these traditional enemies of her people; before Brown Bear and me, both whites; and before timid, frightened White Bear whom she obviously bullied? And what made her finally assent? I would have liked to know the answers to all these questions, but one never knows another quite that well.

Abruptly she broke out into a long harangue in fluent Navajo, then said tersely in English to Brown Bear. "Give her the tea!"

We all sat down to wait while the steam from the cup in the woman's lap rose languidly in the lamplight. "Let's see if she drinks it," said Elizabeth. Whether she did or not, the battle was over. Elizabeth's mood was evaporating like the fragrant tea. The glint in her eyes softened. I suddenly felt a profound respect and affection for this indomitable woman.

When I next glanced at the ailing Navajo woman, she was

bent over a spoonful of tea, inhaling its fragrance with her narrow pinched nostrils and gingerly moistening her thin colorless lips. How sallow her face was, contrasted with the brilliantly striped blanket over her shoulders and the fawn-pink moccasins protruding from it. Perhaps, badly as she needed food and warmth, she needed the assurance of friendship more.

"Oswald!" commanded Elizabeth. "You run over to Richard's right now!"

White Bear threw her a dark look of protest. He resented the way she always called him Oswald, and he hated Navajos. But he grabbed up his hat and flung out into the snow to bring Richard, the medicine-man.

The three Navajo men immediately began an argument in their own tongue. It was ended by one of the sons running out of the door after White Bear. Patiently the father explained that he had sent his son to tell the medicine man not to come until morning; the witch's spell was powerful at night and could not be broken until sun-up. In a little while White Bear and the Navajo returned, saying that Richard would come in the morning. The patient meanwhile had drunk her tea and seemed to be breathing more easily. A little color had come into her hollow checks and the heat of the stove was making her drowsy.

Elizabeth calmly accepted the inevitable. "Oswald, open up the back room! Spread blankets on both beds. They can all stay here tonight."

A few minutes after the Navajos were closed in their room, the two Bears and I left. At noon the next day when I walked to the post office, I saw the pickup driving out of town; presumably the woman's spell had been broken. So had the spell cast upon White Bear, for when I next met him he was placid and affable as ever. Neither of us ever discussed the incident again.

Witchcraft, the power of the evil eye, has a long and proud tradition. In the long ago when the migrating Hopis were living near the red gash of Canyon de Chelly, they initiated a powerful religious ceremony. It was called the Ya Ya from the call announcing the presence of its deity, "Ya-hi-hi! Ya-hi-hi!" Its magic power was invoked from the animal kingdom, *Tuvosi,* Animals With Horns.

Later the people settled down for many years in a village which they called Chipiya, Home of the Mountain Sheep, from the chief of the horned animals. The Ya Ya by now was a great formal ceremony. Its power was very great. Its participants could see far distances and in the dark, as animals; they could see objects sealed up in pottery jars, and many other things invisible to human eyes. Hence from *tuvosi* (animals with horns) and *posi* (eye) derived the Hopi names for a medicine man, a *tuhika* or *posi.*

The symbolism is plain. The animal kingdom is of course the realm of animal instinct within us. Horned animals throughout the world long have been regarded as sacred. To Buddhists the horn symbolized the psycho-physical outgrowth of the ordinary brain center—the so-called Third Eye. Hence the horned antelope pictured on their temples, and the horn trumpet used to call priests in Tibet. The power of supernatural vision we recognize at once as being achieved by the bright eye of intuition.

Soon after the Hopis moved to their present villages, this bright eye clouded over; some of the participants in the Ya Ya were using its power for selfish purposes. Before long they were afflicted with a disease of the eyes. So the practitioners were forced to discontinue the ceremony under threat of banishment.

Yet there were among them some who still secretly used the dark eye of the animal kingdom for evil purposes. Today this growing host of witches and sorcerers are the *powaqa,* who are

119

also known as Two Hearts because they have both human and animal hearts. They gain new members by witching others. A *powaqa* will appear before an innocent person, demanding that he choose between a skull, an ear of corn, a fruit, and a flower. The victim, frightened by the sight of a human skull, usually chooses one of the other objects. He is then told he will die unless he becomes a *powaqa* or designates another member of his family.

With these new members the *powaqa* fly at night, in the dark of the moon, to Palangwu, the high red rock cliff near the mouth of Cayon de Chelly where their first ceremony was anciently performed. The name derives from the word *Pangwu* for the Big Horn Sheep, leader of the animal kingdom. Here in a great kiva inside the cliff is the rendezvous of *powaqa* from all over the world. Each jumps through a hoop which turns him into an animal and gives him the power of its dark eye.

Powaqa bring misfortune and evil to others—destroying crops, bringing winds, driving away snow and rain, and shooting ants, insects, hairs, bones, and glass into their victims. The most evil of all live off the lives of others. They must periodically cause the death of one of their own relatives in order to prolong their own lives.

Who they are no one knows, there are so many of them. There are *powaqa* of both sexes, in all clans, in almost every family. One does not know which of his neighbors, which of his own brothers and sisters, is a *powaqa* bent on taking his own life. So the fear of the dark, evil eye keeps etching deeper every year into Hopi life. Witchcraft today is a unique and distinguishing mark of Hopi life, the obverse and negative side of the great structure of Hopi ceremonialism.

It is wholly consistent that witchcraft became prevalent here about the same time that ceremonialism began to break down—a time coinciding with the arrival of the whites who brought government restrictions and missionary churches; and that its disastrous growth has kept pace with the attrition of traditional religious belief. Witchcraft is but ceremonialism forced underground and perverted by the pressures of modern life which offer no alternative, acceptable belief. Both spring from the same valid source: the animal kingdom, with its instinctive forces of nature, which lies within us and is projected in either its positive or negative aspect.

Navajo ceremonialism also notably accentuates man's relationship to the animal kingdom. In the great ceremony, Mountain Way, held always within its "dark circle of boughs," so aptly named, the mythical hero embodies the bear. Beauty Way symbolically emphasizes snakes, Flint Way the buffalo, Coyote Way the coyote. All interlock in Life Way, the one supreme way of life itself which rises from the unconscious to consciousness. If these dual halves of each man's being are not reconciled, the imbalance results in illness. So each of these ceremonies is conducted to heal an illness by restoring the psychical balance. Today, as among the Hopis, these traditional Sings or Ways are disappearing one by one; and Witchcraft Way is being followed by aberrant Singers or medicine men who use their powers for personal ends—for "soft goods" of blankets and pelts, and "hard goods" of turquoise and silver.

Hopi and Navajo witchcraft to us possess the advantages of a colorful novelty as seen from a safe distance, of a primitiveness we supposedly have left far behind. Or have we? In the Rituale Romanum published by Benziger Brothers in New York in 1947, and endorsed by the coat of arms and introductory letter of Francis Cardinal Spellman, we find, in Latin, detailed instructions for priests to follow in exorcising the devil out of afflicted patients.

121

This astounding primitiveness in our own enlightened society also has deep roots in the past.

The witchcraft frenzy that rose out of medieval Christianity, swept through western Europe and leapt the sea to America, is all too familiar. It lasted for two centuries—from the bull of Pope Innocent VIII validating the persecution of witches in 1484, to the witchcraft trials in Salem in 1692. The amply documented details of the cold-blooded murder of a quarter-million victims attest a holocaust of persecution, torture on the rack, and burning at the stake, whose savagery was never equalled by any tribe of Indians on this continent.

It is pertinent to inquire just what forces impelled this organized massacre. An authority on the history of witchcraft, Rossell Hope Robbins, differentiates between sorcery and witchcraft. Sorcery throughout the world always has been an effort to control natural forces for either good or evil. Witchcraft, which includes the practice of sorcery, is in general a form of religion heretical to orthodox belief. Obviously this multitude of victims, most of them innocent women and children, were not practicing sorcery, witchery, or the black art of demonology. They were condemned to death on the suspicion that they did not adhere to the orthodox belief of the time, medieval Christianity. The essence of witchery, as we shall see, is the projection of the repressed dark forces of the unconscious by one individual or a people upon another. Hence the actual witches were the members of the whole society who seemed to have been suddenly possessed by long accumulated unconscious forces which they projected on their innocent victims.

Witch hunting was instigated by the clergy of the church, both Protestant and Catholic, and then taken over in the name of reason by civil authorities, lawyers and judges, who gradually recognized it as a form of government. Growing in size and intensity as feudalism gave way to capitalism, witch hunting developed stature as an industry. The property of persons accused of witchcraft together with that of their relatives was promptly confiscated. Everyone shared in the profits—the king, nobles, town officials, secular and ecclesiastical courts, the torturers, workmen erecting the scaffolds and stakes, even the shopkeepers and innkeepers thriving on the crowds. The holocaust took on an aspect of what would soon be called Big Business and Big Government. It ended, as Robbins observes, only with the end of feudalism. "Commerce could not live in a world where inquisitorial proceedings could be taken against a man long dead and his property confiscated from his heirs. Businessmen could not put up with a world in which commercial agreements could be capriciously nullified at a whisper of heresy."

The similarity of conditions that gave rise to Hopi witchcraft and European witch hunting is apparent. For Hopi witchcraft too rose out of, but was heretical to, the traditional religion; and spread swiftly as primitive Hopi feudalism gave way to encroaching capitalism in the form of automobile roads, trading posts, hamburger stands, filling stations, and the economic pressures of modern life. The difference is that there is no witch hunting because of the debilitation of orthodox Hopi ceremonialism and society. Hopi witchcraft, alarmingly spreading, is but the last ineffectual mechanism for warding off the encroachment of white society.

Yet again in this century the European pattern of witch hunting was repeated in Germany. Those of us who recall the strident radio voice of Hitler cannot doubt that he was a supreme *powaqa* "wielding an irresistible influence or power more than natural," as Webster defines the power of a witch; and that the Nazi massacre of six million Jews in five years embodied the essence of witchery as practiced by professed witch hunters. The extermination was justified as practical politics and recognized again as a form of government—government by an exclusive, Aryan, master race.

The Nazis did not recognize Christianity; they were possessed by their Teutonic heritage in their rejuvenation of this ancient mythology. All four of the Nazi leaders dressed in Teutonic armor when they met in secret sessions. These meetings were actually Sabbats of witches, for Hitler, Hess, Goebels, and Haushofer were quite aware of the technique of psychological projection. And all Germany welcomed the domination of its warlock leaders. Something deep in the soul of the people responded instantly to the evocation of their mythological past.

The inner self within each one of us presents two opposing aspects, as Jung discovered: one of which might be described as the luminescent divine, and the other its dark luciferian shadow, both embodying psychic energy that may be released for good or evil. Modern man, with his extroverted rationality and his almost complete reliance upon materiality, long had kept repressing into the unconscious the shadow side of his dual nature with all its pent-up energy. And this was what finally burst forth to possess the soul of Germany at Hitler's call, the demonic forces of its archetypal gods under Thor and Wotan rushing toward another Gotter-dammerung.

Let us ask ourselves if what is happening now in this tragic present bears any resemblance to the past. Is the bright eye of intuition clouding over, and the dark eye of the animal kingdom shining forth?

Certainly the mystical elements of early Christianity are lacking in our rationalized religion today. Belief in an orthodox creed is often accepted as a prerequisite to faith. The Church, the great denominational-political-economic institution it has become, has interposed between the individual and his God, forgetting that the birthplace of faith is not the rationally prescribed dogma but the spontaneous religious experience in the individual human soul. We are futilely breasting the ever-rising tide of technology and materialism, bewitched by the TV commercial urging upon us still more senseless gadgets to clutter our crowded lives. We are still losing our individuality as conformity becomes the norm. The danger of man's no longer being Man but Mass Man, a repetitious duplication of millions like him, is yet ominous. The rise of political absolutism owes its success to the promulgation of this mass hypnosis. Whether it be the Third Reich of Hitler's Germany, the Fascists of Mussolini's Italy, the Peronistas of Argentine, or the Communist Party of the Soviet Union and Red China, the omnipotent totalitarian state has been assuming the prerogatives of both nature and religion, exercising complete domination over its unresisting populations.

The course of witchcraft whether practiced by witches or witch hunters is first the possession of them by the dark shadow side of their dual nature they have repressed, and then their projection of it upon another individual, race, or nation. All our fears and faults we see only in other persons, creeds, and political entities, just as they in turn project their inner ills upon us. War and extermination are no cure, as we have found out. Our own almost complete extermination of the red race under the national witch-hunt slogan, "The only good Indian is a dead Indian," has left us a hangover worse than our original drunkenness, a psychotic prejudice against all races of darker skin—the red, the black, the yellow, the brown—whose tragic consequences we are now beginning to suffer. Jews under Hitler, capitalists under Stalin, Communists under McCarthy, all have successively occupied the position of accused witches as in sixteenth- and seventeenth-century Europe. If the mere shadow of suspicion were enough to convict them then, we here have achieved the phrase if not the actuality of guilt by association.

If this continuing projection of our unadmitted dark selves upon others is a form of witchcraft, and I believe it is, we can at least take some comfort in realizing what it is and how to combat it. The dark eye of the animal kingdom within us is also the bright eye of intuition that can, if we will, lead us again out of the gathering darkness.

11. THE SEVEN CAVES

Of all the odd characters in New Oraibi the strangest was an old crippled man, neatly dressed in a black suit, who limped down the road with a cane. Tuwaletstiwa, Sun Standing Up, was his Hopi name, but he was commonly known as Mysterious Mr. Johnson. Believed to possess mystic powers, he was the last leader and one of the two surviving members of the mysterious and powerful Bow Clan.

It was related that many years ago when he was a young man, he and a companion set off from Old Oraibi on horseback to attend a dance in a nearby village. On the way Tuwaletstiwa proposed that each of them break a leg and heal it in order to prove their powers. His companion refused. A few moments later a strange thing occurred. Tuwaletstiwa's horse bolted, throwing him off and breaking his leg. Tuwaletstiwa was unable to heal it, and began limping through life with a cane. Shortly thereafter he turned Christian, moved down to New Oraibi, and began to use the name of Mr. Johnson.

Then a dreadful thing happened. He was seen carrying down the road, publicly exposed to view, the Bow Clan altar. Heedless of the crowd of Hopis, Navajos, and whites gathering to watch him with shocked amazement, he set it up in the middle of the dusty road in front of the trading post. Meticulously he arranged in perfect order all the ritual paraphernalia including the two huge elk horns and the three *mongkos* symbolizing the supreme spiritual power and authority: the six-foot-long *mongko*, the one-foot-long *mongko*, and the most sacred, tiny *mongko* which the Bow Clan had brought from the preceding Third World. Then he lit a match to it.

Lorenzo Hubbell burst out of his trading post, offering $500 for the altar. Mr. Johnson refused. Hubbell then offered him $300 for permission to photograph it before it was destroyed.

127

Again he refused. By now the altar was wreathed in flames. All the Hopis, frightened and horrified, rushed to their homes and closed the doors. The flames mounted and died, changing to a pillar of smoke—all that remained of an altar and a ritual that had been at once the most famous and infamous in all Hopi ceremonialism.

White Bear and I saw Mysterious Mr. Johnson often. Almost daily he limped with his cane and his tortured face down the road to the trading post from his little hut on the lower slope of the rocky mesa. He drove with us once to Moencopi and came to the house several times for supper. He spoke good English, talked well but guardedly, and had an intellectual alertness unusual for a man so old. We wanted him, of course, to relate the whole history of his mysterious and powerful Bow Clan. It had been the leading clan in the Third World; had conducted its ceremonies in the mysterious edifice on Mesa Verde, Colorado, whose ruin is now known as the Sun Temple; and after arriving in Oraibi, it had controlled the rites of the Two Horn and One Horn societies. Mr. Johnson deferred and will probably carry his secrets to his grave.

He did relate to us, however, that upon arriving in this new Fourth World his people had first lived in seven *puesivi* or caves. Then as the people migrated northward they established seven successive villages named after the seven original caves or settlements collectively known as Pupsövi. The villages were Pamosi; Waki; Taiowa, near present Mexico City; Pavati; Hopaqa; Wikima; and Alosaka, which he said had been near the Meteor Crater in Arizona.

His allusion to a Hopi origin or ancestral home in seven caves on this continent was new to me. Yet the myth of seven womb-caverns, caves, or ravines was perhaps as old as the continent itself. The oldest book in America, the sacred *Popul Vuh* of the

128

Quiché Mayas, states that the ancestors of the Mayas originated in seven great ravines. Ancient Aztec migration legends similarly relate the tradition that the Aztecs came from seven caves which lay to the north. The hill of Cuauhyacac held one of the caves whose other names were Tzinacanoztoc, Quauhyacac, Oztoticpac, Huexotla, Cohuatlichan, and Tlallanoztoc. Whatever they all were, actual caves, ravines, or ancestral tribal settlements, the myth awakened a ready response in the first white men to arrive in America.

In fifteenth-century Spain and Portugal there was current a myth relating that in 734, the year Spain was conquered by the infidel Moors, seven fleeing Christian bishops had sailed westward into the Sea of Darkness. In it they found an island on which each prelate established a city that shone with golden radiance. Just where Antillia or *Septe Citate,* the Island of the Seven Cities, was, no mariner knew. It was reported to be not more than two hundred leagues due west from the Canaries and Azores, and the holy radiance of the seven golden cities continued to glow in the minds of men.

Columbus' official discovery of the New World lent more credence to the myth. The greedy Spanish conquerors of Mexico immediately presumed to find a relationship between their own mythical seven cities and the seven cavern-wombs of Aztec tradition. So prompted, an expedition under Coronado set forth from Mexico City in 1540 to seek the golden Seven Cities of Cibola far to the north. What the Spaniards found were merely seven golden-colored adobe villages, now believed to have occupied the site of Zuñi, New Mexico, six of whose names they reported to be: Halona, Hawikuh, Matsaki, Kiakima, Kwakina, and Kianawa.

A strange myth indeed to endure more than four centuries

and suddenly emerge again from the lips of Mysterious Mr. Johnson! What were these seven caves, settlements, or ruined cities; and if they really existed, where were they?

My interest in them was not entirely bookish. Twenty-five years before, I had ridden a weekly one-car train up the course of the Yaqui River in Sonora, Mexico to the old settlement of Tonichi. From here I had ridden horseback with three Yaquis farther and higher into the wilderness of the Sierra Madre. Why I was there and where I was going, I did not know. It is only youth that believes the secret of life lies just over the next mysterious range of mountains rather than in the more mysterious wilderness within us. Perhaps it was the legendary seven Yaqui villages that drew me, six of which Padre Kino had marked on his map of 1701: Potam, Rahum, Vicam, Torin, Bacum, and Cacorim. Always that mythical seven, even here among the Yaquis.

We pushed on, living on an occasional deer or *javelina* shot in the chaparral. To Bacanora, famous among the people of those hills for the strong mescal named after it. To Sahuaripa, fronting the crest of the sierras that marked the line between Sonora and Chihuahua. There we ran into a stray band of Tarahumaras who described a maze of seven mighty *barrancas,* or canyons, that cut through the backbone of the Sierra Madre south of us in Chihuahua. It was so deep that when snow whitened the rimrock tropical life still thrived at the bottom—oranges and lemons, parrots and strange birds, queer animals. Few people other than the Tarahumaras had ever seen it, it was so inaccessible, but here in its fastnesses were hidden their ancestral villages. The very appearance of these Tarahumaras, almost naked, with long uncombed hair, seemed to justify their words.

It was enough! Could these seven mysterious *barrancas* be the mythical seven womb-caverns of the Aztecs and Mayas? But my Yaqui companions refused to go farther. The Continental Divide was too rugged to traverse without pack animals loaded with adequate supplies. Reluctantly, with one last look at that smoke-blue range, I turned back.

It has always seemed strange to me that however deep we repress our secret desires, life someday brings them to surface. Now, a quarter of a century later, shortly after Mysterious Mr. Johnson reawakened my interest in the myth, Brice Sewell asked me to accompany him on a trip to Chihuahua. Brice had been an Indian trader among the Pueblos and Navajos for many years and was becoming interested in the Tarahumaras, reputed to be the wildest, most primitive, and least known tribe in all Mexico. In order to establish better contact with them, he also invited Jose Abeyta, the cacique or religious leader of San Juan Pueblo in New Mexico. Jose was a little man of seventy who wore his hair in two long pigtails. Mindful of the importance of his trip, he carried a little buckskin pouch filled with sacred cornmeal with which he could offer prayers on due occasion. So late in October, riding in a sturdy old Chevy, we struck off on our busman's holiday.

At Chihuahua City we turned west and reached the end of the road at the little 300-year-old town of Ciudad Guerrero. Deep in the Sierra Madre beyond it lay Sisoguichi, a Tarahumara mission established by the Jesuits. The road was unmarked and dangerous, but a friend, Guillermo Gonzales, found us a driver who felt confident he could make it. He was a brawny young man named Umberto Frias, a superb driver and a jolly companion. So once again, with a strange feeling of entering familiar country, we began climbing into the sierras.

Without Umberto we could never have found the road nor driven the car over it. Double-clutching all the way to inch the axles over high rocky centers and rolling boulders out of the way, we reached the crest of one range only to confront another. Fording rivers and streams demanded an agony of effort. The car would sink in icy water, requiring all four of us to strip off our pants and shoes, jack up the car under water, and then pry it out with poles.

This was the region I had wanted to cross years ago, a wilderness of high forested ranges seamed with rocky gorges and deep canyons. Not until we crossed the Continental Divide did we see any sign of life save an occasional hut fronting a *milpa* of squaw corn. Just below it lay Bacoyna, a frontier settlement where we siphoned out gas from a huge storage tank and ate tortillas, beans, and eggs in a cafe where chickens ran across the dirt floor. We might have been back home in the Navajo and Hopi country of a century ago.

Late that afternoon we reached Sisoguichi—the first passenger car, we were told, to enter the mission grounds. The eighty-five-mile trip had taken us eleven hours. The Tarahumara mission was imposingly modern: a large church, hospital, boarding school for Tarahumara children, a leatherwork shop, and even a radio station, XEUS. One of its twelve priests, Padre Ernesto Urgana, who conducted us through the mission, said that there were about 60,000 Tarahumaras in this wild mountain region. They lived in caves or tiny villages, growing corn and raising small flocks of goats; a Stone Age life marked with ignorance, poverty, and disease. The mission here was their only contact with the outside world, but all this would soon change; a new railway was being built across the sierras which would open the area to progress. Everything about the mission seemed oddly familiar; it reminded us of Ganado Mission in the heart of the Navajo country back home.

There was no room for us in the compound, but we were

shown a house outside where we could get a supper of eggs, beans, and tortillas. Afterward we were conducted to our sleeping quarters—two small rooms in another adobe hut across the road. Crouching here in bitter cold, by the guttering light of a candle, we talked until midnight with the Tarahumaras who came to call at Jose's invitation. Then we rolled up in our sleeping bags on the dirt floor and helplessly gave ourselves up to the swarms of fleas.

Jose's long, braided hair and the little buckskin pouch worn at his breast, opened the door to the Tarahumaras for us. But not very far. Like all mission Indians they were wary of talking about their primitive and pagan background in front of any member of the mission staff. But alone, and with other small groups straggling in from the trails beyond the compound, they were fascinated by Jose's descriptions of his own people's beliefs, customs and ceremonies, and told us some of their own.

The Tarahumaras' own name for themselves was Raramuri, compounded of the words *rara* for "foot" and *juma,* "to run." Like the Hopis, the men were famed long-distance runners, able to cover a hundred miles without stopping, and accustomed to running down a deer until it was exhausted. Almost all their religious and social gatherings featured races: the men kicking a small wooden ball over long courses, and the women racers using a hoop and stick similar to the hoop and ball used by Hopi women. The Tarahumaras, like the Hopis, were corn-eaters. On the trail they relied on *pinole,* roasted and ground corn mixed with water, or *atole,* the same mixture boiled into a gruel. At every gathering *tesguino,* a corn beer, was served.

Each village was governed by a cacique or chief known as the Sedigma or Seligame, derived from the word *selaka* for the lance he carried as a mark of his authority. Their *hechizero,* the medicine man or witch doctor, used a crystal for seeing internal ills and cured his patients with preparations of herbs. Such shamans were known as Oorugame. The Tarahumaras' own ceremonial dance, accompanied by chanting and rattling, they called a *dutuburi*. It was followed next morning by a *yumari*, the most important being held on May 3. Like the Pueblos back home they also danced the *Matachines*, adopted from the Spanish.

Undoubtedly the Tarahumaras were the purest, most primitive, and least-known tribe in Mexico. Although they had a tradition that they came from the north, their origin was unknown. At Citahuichic, the ancient Tarahumaras' Place of Reunion, I had made a drawing of one of the pictographs carved on the rocks along the bank of the Rio Papigochic. Jose could not interpret it, nor did any of the Tarahumaras we met identify it.

In addition to the many striking similarities between the Hopis and Tarahumaras, both tribes were included in the Uto-Aztecan linguistic group; and I wished we had brought along John Lansa to compare the two languages. But he did not speak Spanish as did Jose, who found no similarity between Tarahumara and his own Tewa tongue. Most of the Tarahumara place-names ended in "chi"—Sisoguichi, Bahuinocahchi, Rechaguachi; or in "chic"— Papigochic, Temechic, Cocomorachic. Evidently the very name of Chihuahua was of Tarahumara origin, indicating their occupation of the entire state in prehistoric times. Today, wild and aloof, they have retreated into the remote and trackless *barrancas* and sierras. From here they travel everywhere throughout northern Mexico; one sees a lone runner or a straggling family wandering up into Sonora or even down to Chihuahua City to stand forlornly on a street corner, as do our own Navajos in Gallup.

What struck me with peculiar significance during these talks was that the Tarahumaras' ancestral home lay in the unknown heart of the vast wilderness of the Sierra Madre, the maze of seven canyons known as the Barranca de Cobre. Here it was again, the seven womb-caverns. Moreover the great Barranca was not far away. We had only to drive to the frontier town of Creel, and thence about thirty miles to the edge of the Barranca itself.

Hopefully we started out again on an almost indiscernible, tortuous road bestrewn with jagged rock and boulders. After an hour's struggle we gave up and wearily turned back, hoping to reach Ciudad Guerrero before the car burned out.

Back at Pumpkin Seed Point, I showed the photograph and drawing of the pictograph we had found along the Rio Papigochic to some of our informants. They identified it as a signature of the Water Clan. I also described the ruins of Casas Grandes which Brice, Jose, and I had visited on our way home. This great complex of ruins comprised a truncated pyramid, ball court, three huge mounds shaped like a snake, a parrot, and a cross, and hundreds of well-laid-out rooms surrounding a central plaza. This ancient metropolis had just been jointly excavated by the National Institute of Anthropology and History of Mexico and by the Amerind Foundation in Arizona, and is reported to have been of Toltec origin, dating back to 850 A.D. Obviously Casas Grandes lay almost midway on a migratory or trade route between the later Aztec capital to the south and the Great Pueblos to the north, and it comprised features of both cultures. What the purpose of the mounds had been evidently was not known, but our Hopi spokesmen described in careful detail one of the ceremonies for which it had been used. How did they know? They insisted simply that Hopi clans had occupied Casas Grandes during their migration northward from the Seven Caves.

All these observations posed a plethora of questions. If the mythical seven womb-caverns of the Aztecs lay to the north of present Mexico City, and those of the Hopis lay to the south of their present villages in northern Arizona, they undoubtedly existed somewhere between, in northern Mexico. Could they have been the maze of seven great *barrancas* or canyons now generally known as the Barranca de Cobre in the mountain wilderness of Chihuahua? The many similarities between the Hopis and the Tarahumaras in appearance, customs, and beliefs were too striking to be ignored. Were they branches of the same family tree which had been rooted here? But what related the myths of seven cities as held by the Yaquis, the Zuñis, and the Portuguese and Spaniards long before the discovery of this New World? These questions apparently lay in the fields of documentary ethnology and anthropology.

As I sat at Pumpkin Seed Point watching Otto Pentiwa clatter down the road behind his old nag, followed by Mysterious Mr. Johnson limping with his cane in a swirl of dust, the fallacy of seeking an objective answer to a subjective question was immediately apparent. For myth is not based upon rational fact. Expressing as no other medium the deepest truths of life, it wells up within us in the same involuntary processes which shape the mind, the foetus within the womb, the cells within a crystal. How then can one ever discover its meaning by sailing across an unknown sea, plodding through the wilderness of a strange new continent? Its truth can be found only by exploring a mythic and symbolic level below the surface of scientifically observable fact. At least my own topographical explorations were over, my own immature questions answered.

The thousand-year-old myth of the seven cities, the seven caves, belongs to all mankind. They all lie within that vast sea of darkness in man himself; the womb-caverns of the unconscious whence the soul begins its migratory journey into the light of consciousness. This is the golden radiance that enwrapped the *Septe Citate* of the early Spanish and Portuguese mariners, the golden sheen reflected from the adobe walls of the Seven Cities of Cibola first glimpsed by Fray Marcos, the radiant truth intuitively glimpsed by every man who confronts the unknown wilderness within him.

Man's journey into the interior is not to be undertaken lightly. This is the realm of the inexpressible, mysterious divinity of life. It is not a coincidence that the island of the *Septe Citate* was reputedly discovered by Christian bishops, and that knowledge of the mythical Pupsövi of the Hopis had been confined to ceremonial leaders like Mr. Johnson. The same aura of sanctity envelopes them all.

The lowest of the psychophysical centers within the human body, as recognized by the Hopis, is known as the "Throne of the Creator"—the seat of the sun in man, the *solar plexus.* The highest is the soft spot at the crown of the head, the *kopavi* or "Open Door" to the Creator enthroned in the heavens above. These two thrones for the sun and the Creator present no paradox if man's body is but a microcosmic replica of the macrocosmic body of all creation as held by the ancient Toltecs and Aztecs.

The Zuñi variant is much the same. All their cave-wombs or underworlds are embodied within the Mother of Creation and from them man has been successively reborn. From the Place of Generation mankind first emerged to the second dark cave-world, located near the navel of the Earth Mother and hence called the Umbilical Womb or Place of Gestation. The third cave-world was lighter, "like a valley in starlight," and named the Vaginal Womb or Place of Sex-Generation. In the fourth world-cave, the Womb of Parturition, it was "light like the dawning" and men began to perceive according to their natures. Finally mankind emerged into *Tek'ohaian Ulahname,* the World of Disseminated Light and Knowledge of the Sun Father himself—the ascent to the Fifth World first made by the mythical Quetzalcoatl.

Western medical science recognizes seven physical centers in man, ascending upward from the base of the spine to the brain: the *sacral plexus, plexus pelvis, solar plexus, sympaticus plexus* or heart, *plexus cervicus,* the *medulla oblongata,* and the pituitary gland of the brain.

The mystery teachings of India and Tibet define the locations and functions of seven centers or *chakras* which roughly correspond to these physical centers but are not identified with them, because they function psychically as well as physiologically. The psychologist Dr. Jacobi asserts the *chakras* are centers of psychic energy. Jung believed, like the Eastern sages, that they are centers of consciousness. The seventh and most important *chakra,* known as the Thousand Petalled Lotus, lies, like the Hopi *kopavi,* just below the crown of the head and is regarded as the seat of universal consciousness.

Man throughout his evolutionary development is predominantly controlled by each of these centers in turn, which successively become less gross and more subtle in function during his ascent in consciousness. At the final stage he attains universal consciousness and his physical evolution on the material plane ends. The mystery teachings assert, however, that he need not endure eons of development through countless life-forms to reach this eventual goal. Under strict disciplines man in one lifetime can direct his psychic forces up through the lower six centers to the seventh and experience that light of supramundane consciousness termed enlightenment or illumination.

The gradual emergence of universal consciousness from the darkness of matter that veils it is the Toltec and Aztec, the Hopi and Zuñi Road of Life up through their successive underworlds. It is the long journey of mankind—a journey that takes place within man himself, as Quetzalcoatl taught.

The *Septe Citate* of the early Portuguese and Spanish, the golden Seven Cities of Cibola, the seven ravines of the Quiché Maya, the seven womb-caverns of the Aztecs, the seven ancestral *barrancas* of the Tarahumaras, the seven caves of the Hopis, the seven womb-caves of the Zuñis, and the seven ancestral villages of the Yaquis—all these can be equated with the seven psycho-physical centers within man himself. Primitive as man may be, he always has divined their existence, and their faint glimmer in his abysmal darkness takes on all the shapes of his imagination. By them he gropes his way to the final Self, of whose transcendent illumination these are but dim reflections.

12. THE CANYON OF MYSTERY

In the floor of every Hopi kiva there is a small hole called the *sipapuni*. Etymologically derived from the two words for "navel" and "path from," the *sipapuni* symbolizes the umbilical cord leading from the Mother of Creation, the place of man's Emergence from the underworld, the entrance to the womb of life. In the small plaza at Old Oraibi in front of the Snake Kiva, known as Tipkyavi, the Womb, there is another *sipapuni*. The supreme symbol for this place of beginning lies ninety miles west. It is the phenomenal mile-deep gash down through all our geological eras to the two-billion-year-old Archeozoic rock system, part of the original earth's crust—the majestic and sublime Grand Canyon. Here at its bottom lies the last and deepest *sipapuni* of all.

The significance of the *sipapuni* is dramatically emphasized early in the fall during the Wuwuchim ceremony when novices participate in an enactment of the Emergence as a part of their initiation. Their initiation is not complete, however, until they make a pilgrimage to Grand Canyon the following spring. Failing to complete this they remain *kekelt*, fledgling hawks too spiritually weak to fly. The journey is long, arduous, and dangerous. The leader selected to guide the young hawks is a mature man with a pure heart. Each carries a pouch of sacred cornmeal, several *pahos* to plant at the shrines, and a supply of cooked dried corn, dried peaches, and *piki* for food. Although the trip must be made on foot, several burros are taken along to bring back the rock salt the men will gather in the Salt Cave at the bottom of the Canyon.

The ancient route leads across the desert, through twelve great sand dunes, and over the rising mesa to the sheer edge of Grand Canyon. Here, near the shrine of Salt Woman, two men are left to take care of the burros and to pray for the success of the others who make the dangerous climb down the cliff walls with ropes. At the river's edge below is a natural mound of earth about three feet high and three feet in diameter, called the kiva, at whose bottom is a well of clear, still water, the *sipapuni*. Carefully the young hawks drop in their prayer-feathers. The leader calls to the spirits within, "Wake up! Why are you asleep?" In immediate answer a geyser of hot water and mud erupts. As it subsides, the water sucks under the *pahos* of the young hawks who have had good thoughts, indicating that their prayers will be answered. Others still float on the surface as a sign of their rejection. Not far away is another small opening into which the men thrust their arms, depositing *pahos* and bringing out handsful of *pasquapi,* the distinctive blue coloring used for painting ceremonial objects. Finally the men reach the Salt Cave with its stalactites and stalagmites of rock salt, its countless hollows of dripping salt water. This is where they chip off bags of salt to carry home; where they deposit little cornmeal effigies of sheep and horses to harden like rock as a sign their flocks and herds will increase. It is a place of mystery, prayer, and concentration, of strange dreams and visions. For this is the great *sipapuni,* the entrance to the underworld, the womb of life, the noumenal source. The young hawks who survive this tremendous psychic experience and the dangerous climb out are then regarded as having flown off the nest.

One fall at Shongopovi I saw several of these neophytes about to enter the kiva for the first rituals comprising Wuwuchim. They were big, brawny youths with small hawk feathers tied in their hair. Yet as each stepped on the ladder to descend, an old frail man crouched under him to carry him inside, so weak were his spiritual wings. Inexpressibly funny as it looked, the scene drove home the symbolism too vividly to be forgotten. All winter I waited for the new initiates to make their pilgrimage to Grand Canyon so I could learn the dreams and visions they had experienced. They did not go; the trip was now considered too arduous and dangerous. But from several old men came stories of what they had seen and experienced during their own pilgrimages.

Two of them impressed me.

Near the *sipapuni,* at the bottom of the canyon, a group of *kekelt* had come upon a strange imprint in the soft sand. It was as large as a man's foot but shaped like a frog's. Finally the leader spoke. "Clearly," he said, "it is the footprint of Paqua." "Paqua" means "frog" and a man named Paqua lived at Oraibi. Obviously he had just died and left his footprint here where he returned to the underworld. The men's belief was confirmed when they arrived back in Oraibi; Paqua had died during their absence.

The other story was told by several old men, all of whom at the same time had come upon a strange building full of strange objects that vanished next morning. Years later the same scene manifested itself with objective reality as the new trading post at New Oraibi. What they had seen was clearly a vision of the future.

The psychological content of these stories puzzled me: that the spirit of the dead return to the Beginning; that in the archaic past lies the future. There was indeed a great deal about the cryptic meaning of the pilgrimage I did not understand until the following spring when there came for me a sequel to my quest for the seven caves.

Our friend Guillermo Gonzalez in Chihuahua wrote that the new railroad we had heard about at Sisoguichi had just been completed. Named the Ferrocarril Chihuahua al Pacifico, it stretched across the tawny plains of Chihuahua and over the snow-high Sierra Madre mountains to Los Mochis on the semi-tropical, coastal plain of Sinaloa, only twelve miles from the tiny Pacific Coast port of Topolobampo. The insignia chosen for the new line was a Tarahumara runner, and a group of Tarahumara children had participated in its dedication ceremony high on the Alta Sierra Tarahumara. The new *ferrocarril* skirted the awesome Barranca de Cobre, he added, and was now making two trips a week.

Fortunately a large weekly magazine was interested in getting factual and photographic coverage of the line. So I wired Guillermo, asking if he could secure mules and guides so we could descend into the Barranca. Within two weeks arrangements were complete. There were four of us who finally met at Los Mochis for the trip: Bill Bridges, a photographer from Los Angeles; Guillermo; my wife, Rose; and myself.

Los Mochis was a huge sugar mill set in a modern town surrounded by unbroken expanses of waving sugar cane. A taxi-drive away, little-known Topolobampo looked down on its placid and hill-rimmed bay. A steep hillside village, its tiny plaza swarmed with happy, unspoiled people. Here we found preposterously excellent seafood brought from the best fishing waters in the world. We chose from corbina and cabrillo, red snappers, tutoavas, shrimp, turtle, and yellowtail.

It had been a long time since three of us had seen the sea; and waiting for the day the train was to leave, we took a launch out through the blue, watery valley into the Sea of Cortez, as fisherfolk still call the Gulf of California. Twelve miles out there loomed up what appeared to be a solitary huge chunk of chocolate cake encrusted with caramel icing. It was the 456-foot-high, rocky promontory of El Faralon surrounded by leaping tortoises and swarming with hundreds of seals and sea lions, thousands of screaming birds. If it was a long way from parched-brown, barren Pumpkin Seed Point, it seemed even farther from that awesome chasm gaping soft and mysterious in sunlight and silence deep in the Sierra Madre. Yet even out here at sea the Barranca cast its spell. One of the boatmen told us the widespread legend that sea lions from El

Faralon travel up the Urique River to the bottom of the Barranca.

Their hollow, coughing bark echoing as no other sound the deep-throated, resonant voice of the sea; the vast expanses of sugar cane swarming with countless migrating flocks of wild duck and geese; the wide valley of the Fuerte lush with bananas, mangoes, papayas, oranges, and limes; the sea, the land, the very air itself denied the existence of an impalpable mystery which could exert such a pull of gravity upon us.

"Are you sure mule-drivers and their animals will meet us?" we kept asking Guillermo.

Guillermo was young, small, and lightly boned, with a touch of the arrogance so amply displayed by his aristocratic Spanish forebears, owners of the immense Amaya hacienda near Santo Tomas. He flicked the dust off his boots and smiled sharply. "Cómo no?"

We bought supplies: ropes and bags, food and cooking utensils, some spare blankets. Rose, who loved the stalls in the old *mercado,* came back with small presents for the Tarahumaras we might meet. Still no one was quite convinced we were really going down into the Barranca. Everyone had heard of it. No one had seen it. Even now, with all the warnings, it still held an air of nebulous unreality exaggerated by the practical modernity of Los Mochis itself.

At last, at six o'clock in the morning, we rushed for the train. It comprised two express cars, three old coaches and pullmans brought down from the United States, and a diner. All were packed with people bound for Mexico's new frontier. We had to secure a second compartment to hold all our luggage and supplies and Bill's photographic equipment. He was a large man weighing more than two hundred pounds, a jolly companion, and a meticulous worker who pried open the grimy windows so he could hang out with his camera and photograph the train snaking around the dizzy curves. By mid-morning we had crossed the beautiful bridge over El Fuerte and were beginning the slow, hard climb through Septentrion Canyon into the Sierra Madre. Slowly its scenic treasures heaped up around us. Mountains overgrown with pipe-organ cactus. Perpendicular cliffs out of whose barren rock grew the strange tree, *texcalama*. Tiny rivers green as liquid soap viscuously curling into white lather around the rocks far below. Once more we were in that vast motherland which stretches north through Arizona and New Mexico and whose spinal vertebrae pinch out in the Sangre de Cristo peaks rearing above my own back pasture. A land that by some strange alchemy reflects—in every ligament and integument, in the warm, dry texture of its skin, in the slow pulse beating deep within—the unique quality of its hidden being. One born to its rhythm recognizes no political boundaries; he feels more at home below the Rio Grande than across the Missouri.

Guillermo was justly proud of this section of the line. It was, he said, one of the great feats of railroad engineering in the world. Its roadbed supported welded sections of steel rail set on concrete ties cushioned by rubber plates. We did not comment on the outmoded rolling stock which brought us up with frequent jerks and rattles, and we could well believe his statistics when we pierced the mountains through seventy-two tunnels, one of which was a mile long, and crossed deep gorges over thirty-nine bridges and nine viaducts.

Still it was the people we passed, more than the scenery and the line itself, who called to the heart; everything reduces to human terms. All through these sierras we could see the miracle of the train reflected in the faces of isolated families who had never seen a wagon, an automobile, or an airplane. A man and a woman in tattered clothes waving to us from a thatched *ramada,* a *jacale,* or crumbling adobe hut. A few Tarahumara children perched on a cliff overhead. All with the wonder and the mystery in their dark eyes. Indians gathered to watch the new iron mule pass by, the great event in their lonely lives here as it had been on our own frontier a century ago.

"Are you sure those damned mules will be there?" persisted Bill. "The train stops only five minutes and there won't be another pass by for four days, you know."

Guillermo shrugged and dusted his boots for the last time.

Finally the moment came that we had long anticipated. It came without warning that afternoon when the train stopped on a high, pine-covered crest at a place known as El Divisadero, "The Lookout." There was no station, no building of any kind, not even a sign. Simply a small clearing with a large wooden cross standing at its far edge. Here the earth abruptly dropped away into an awesome, bare-rock chasm that seemed to have no bottom at all. It was the Barranca.

No one on the train believed our extravagant notion of climbing down into it as we hurriedly unloaded our mountain of baggage in the clearing. Engineer, conductor, porters, and passengers frantically kept waving for us to get back on. They were still waving when the train pulled out. Rose's face wore a look of resigned consternation. Bill was scowling. El Divisadero was far from being another El Tovar on the rim of Grand Canyon.

Guillermo, however, was smiling. A line of mounted men was coming through the pines. They were the *arrieros* who had arrived on time, as he had promised. There were four of them: Roberto and Cecilio Valenguela who had come from the little settlement of Areponapuchi nearby, Ismael Rodriguez from Bacoyna, and a long-haired Tarahumara named Trinidad Molina from Guadalupe y Calvo. All appeared to be quiet, courteous, and competent. I was

146

not so sure of the seven scrawny mules.

A mile away we reached a *ranchito* with an empty cabin. Fortunately its owner, Señor Ingeniero Efrain Sandoval Loera, and three of his men, had just ridden up from Creel, and invited us to sleep on the floor that night. After cooking supper for all twelve of us, we sat around a candle with Señor Sandoval. Sketching a map, he explained that the Barranca was a vast complex of five major canyons. Barranca de Cobre, Barranca de Urique, Barranca de Tararecua, Barranca de Cusarare, and Barranca de Batopila, and two minor canyons, Barranca de Oteros and Barranca de Sinforosa, all draining into the Urique River. This vast system had never been completely surveyed and few explorers had plumbed its tortuous depths, but from various estimates it was a quarter-mile deeper and perhaps twice as long as the 283-mile-long, mile-deep Grand Canyon cut by the Colorado.

Señor Sandoval was a tall, slim man about fifty years old with a soft voice and impeccable manners. He was well educated and widely traveled, and for all the practicality he displayed I began to detect in him a streak of the visionary quality that so often runs through the Spanish character.

"I happen to own the stretch of land here at the rim," he was saying modestly. "It is an advantageous position for it drops down to almost the exact center of the whole *barranca* system—the junction, to be precise, of the Barranca de Cobre, Barranca de Urique, and Barranca de Tararecua, the three main canyons. Most of the few people who have reported seeing it, as you know, have driven from Creel to the old La Bufa mine at the Barranca de Batopila, far to the south of the main complex of chasms. But here begins the trail to its central depths.

"El Divisadero," he continued, "is an ideal location with all the possibilities of the Santa Fe Railroad's famous El Tovar on the south rim of Grand Canyon. It is imperative we in Mexico do something to develop it. My architect is now drawing plans for a similar tourist hotel here with a long balcony overlooking the gorge. It will be strictly modern, in good taste, and patterned after scenic resorts I've seen in the Bavarian Alps. With government cooperation and proper financing, I hope also to add something new. A cable car, modeled somewhat on a ski-chair lift, will run down to the bottom of the *barranca* with perhaps two or three stopping places on the way down." He turned to Rose to say politely, "You would no doubt prefer that, would you not, señora? The present trail is not too well marked, I'm afraid. It will perhaps be a difficult trip."

The cooking fires outside had died down. The men were rolled in their blankets. The night wind was soughing through the pine tips, that immemorial sound of solitude which is as comforting to the mountain-born as the murmur of the surf to seafolk. Soon we were stretched in our sleeping bags on the floor of the cabin.

It was a long time before I went to sleep. Something within me was trying to condense into one integrated, meaningful whole the Grand Canyon and the vaster, deeper Barranca below us; the Hopi pilgrimages and our own somewhat foolhardy and impulsive trip; the subjective meaning of the seven caves and the symbol of the *sipapuni*. At the same time I could hear Guillermo snoring on one side of me and Rose restlessly moving on the other. Out of all this welter of thought and sensation there emerged, side by side, the well-stocked trading post the Hopis had seen in Grand Canyon years before it had been built in New Oraibi, and Señor Sandoval's resplendent tourist hotel with a cable car running down into the Barranca. What little difference there was between these two visions! Then suddenly, as if by the same gravitational pull that had drawn us here, I was sucked down into dreamless sleep.

Early next morning we started down: Guillermo who preferred walking; the four muleteers leading four pack mules; Bill, Rose, and I riding mules respectively named Violeta, Sledgehammer, and Diablo; and a long-haired black goat we had bought at the *ranchito* to butcher that night.

Within a half-hour the shady, soughing pines drew aside to reveal an abysmal cleft in the vast bulks of cactus-studded, brown rocks shimmering in sunlight. This was the "stupendous gorge" described in 1684 by the indomitable Jesuit, Padre Juan Maria Salvatierra, the first European to see it. He got off his mule "on the side opposite the precipice, sweating and trembling all over from fright. For there opened on the left a chasm, the bottom of which could not be seen, and on the right rose perpendicular walls of solid rock."

It seemed likely that no one save Tarahumaras had made the descent here since the Padre. The trail was almost indiscernible: scarcely a foot wide, obstructed by ledges of jagged rock and slides of loose gravel, and zig-zagging in turns almost too sharp for the mules. I felt sorry for Rose as more and more often we had to dismount to lead the mules. But there was no turning back now. We kept dropping at every step.

How different this was from the Bright Angel Trail into Grand Canyon! The Barranca did not have the jagged pinnacles and lofty spires, the bottomless flat-topped buttes and mesas floating so mystically blue in a measureless dimension comprising both space and time, the brilliant red sandstones, the clear green shales, the pure limestone whites, and all their paint-pot tints and shades changing with every change of light. It lacked all the drama of shape and color, of shifting mists and swirling clouds. It simply gaped, soft and mysterious in sunlight and silence, more compelling by its stark barrenness. The quality of this compulsion kept growing as those soft uterine folds of living flesh constricted tighter and tighter, drawing us ever deeper into a bottomless womb. That was the illusion those great bare hills created as they pressed around, above, and behind with their smothering softness and growing shadows, and finally closed behind us.

"*La mula!*" somebody yelled. In an instant the air was thick with cries and curses. A pack mule had slipped, rolled off the trail, and caught on the stump of a tree. Now began the devil's own job of hauling him back. Only to be interrupted a few minutes later by another frightened cry. "*Cuidado! La mujer!*" This time a loose talus slope had given away under Rose. Luckily she had fallen spread-eagle and now lay there unable to move for fear of causing an avalanche.

Always, everywhere, the danger of slipping and plunging into an eternity of softness and silence. It was no place for a woman, especially one with a touch of acrophobia. Nor for a huge man like Bill, weighted down with cameras and lenses which he seemed to treasure more than his own skin. Guillermo was limping badly in his now scuffed and scratched boots. One dared not think of the heaving, sweating mules. But the pitiful bleat of the goat, jerked along by a tether on legs growing too weak to walk, appealed to a heart whose compassion had no outlet. What a hell of a way for a living thing to spend its last day on earth! The trail narrowed. The *arrieros* cut off an obstructing branch of a tree and we continued on.

By early afternoon the gorge had narrowed to a steep pass, the head of a small clear stream. Along it grew from here down to the river the "orchards"—small clumps of orange, lemon, and lime trees planted by the Tarahumaras whose caves in the cliffs we had glimpsed on the way down. Each tree was individually owned, its trunk carved with the sign of its owner. The precious fruit as it ripened he would pack up the steep trail and carry to the nearest settlements in a small bag or basket woven from the fibers of the *sotol.*

Our mule-train as a whole could go no farther. All the animals except one pack mule were turned loose, and the pack saddles and most of the equipment were laboriously hoisted to the high crotch of an enormous wild fig tree to wait overnight. The smooth bark of these great trees the Aztecs had used for the paper, *amatl,* on which were written their codices. Only then did we drop on the ground, almost too exhausted to eat lunch. The Tarahumara refused our hearty fare, stirring up a handful of his *pinole* in a cup of water and drinking slowly.

How wonderful it was to lie in this tropical oasis, watching the large flitting butterflies and little tropical birds. To glimpse the bare, brown bodies of the men ducking under a waterfall. To drink again and again from a tiny spring bubbling out from between the roots of the great fig. But it was a mirage of comfort that could not last.

The long-haired Tarahumara swung the exhausted goat over his shoulders to carry to its death. Two more muleteers packed the remaining mule with supplies for the night and started climbing down the hillside again, one pulling the mule and the other whacking it with a club behind. Another carrying all of Bill's precious camera equipment. And the rest of us sweating behind.

The last descent from the cliffside above the oasis was a torture. How long had it been since other travelers had preceded us? Or was this trail used only by the few Tarahumaras who kept the orchards? For at the bottom there still remained a thick growth of bamboo, willow, and choking brush to cut through with machetes before we finally reached a sandy bar on the bank of the Urique. It was already stained with the blood of the butchered goat.

Our ten hours of struggle was worth it. We had reached the

heart of the Barranca. The spot was the bottom of the Barranca de Urique just below its conjunction with the Barranca de Cobre and Barranca de Tararecua whose waters swelled the Urique into a wide, boulder-strewn river tepid as stale beer.

The elation of our victory faded with the fading light—and swiftly at this great depth, for there is no twilight. The looming cliffs blotted out the sun, and the world suddenly became a shadowy womb-cavern deep in the immortal, maternal earth. Upstream, the cliff walls flanking the narrow gorge appeared to be closed by a ninety-degree rampart higher still. Downstream the river seemed to end at another jutting wall. A strange river that seemed to bubble up from the depths of the earth only to vanish underground again. The flicker of the fire, from which we withdrew after supper to let the exhausted muleteers sleep, did not dispel the illusion. Nor was the smell of the goat's blood splashed on its sacrificial rock any help. It seemed to be drawing swarms of insects to join those that had attacked our legs the moment we rolled up our pants to wade in the river with aching feet. We could only lie scratching our swelling welts and listening for the hollow, coughing bark of the sea lions which presumably had followed us from El Faralon. But all night long we could hear only the tepid water washing over the rocks. Another legend dispelled.

The mystery of the Barranca remained.

Man's compulsion to climb higher and higher mountain peaks is easily understandable. The victory of height is the victory of the phallic church steeple thrusting upward into the sky, the symbol of the freed consciousness reaching toward the light. Like the towering skyscrapers of Manhattan, it is a distinctive mark of our masculine, rational, Christian-European civilization.

Indian America, polarized to the feminine and instinctive forces of life, always has been preoccupied with depth. Its own unique symbol is the cavern-womb in the depths of Mother Earth, the underground kiva and its *sipapuni*. But what is it today that draws so many of us into the Cave of the Winds, the Carlsbad Caverns, the Royal Gorge, the Grand Canyon, and the Barranca, into deep chasms and mammoth caves everywhere? Is it merely the force of gravity that pulls us below surface to an invisible, sea-level mean? Or rather is it a latent urge toward regression—to crawl back into the uterine folds of the womb of our earthmother? To rest once again, as we shall eventually, within the foetal membranes of her who bore us all?

It seemed to me, as I lay at the bottom of what may well be the deepest chasm in America, that its meaning was deeper than this. For consciousness, having once broken free from the maternal unconscious, cannot sink back defeated into the maw of its devouring mother. It must continue to climb toward a still higher level. But man cannot cut himself off from the one great pool of all life itself without losing all that he has gained. Periodically he must return to the depths of his archaic past in the fathomless unconscious: to be renewed by the underground waters of life welling from the noumenal source; to glimpse at the Beginning a vision of the End of his mysterious search. This, it seemed to me as a thin moon curved over the rim of the great wall enclosing us, was the ritual second act of the one great mystery play we all must individually complete before we are psychically mature enough to fly off the nest. It explained the purpose of the Hopi pilgrimage down into Grand Canyon and the meaning of our own increasing preoccupation with depth; there can be no Emergence to a higher consciousness without a Return to the fathomless deeps within us. The thought gave shape to the mysterious quality of that abysmal cleft in the flesh of the living earth in which we slept. It seemed enough that we had endured our descent only to glimpse its vague outline. . . .

Fearful that we might miss the biweekly train, we began our climb back out of the gorge next morning without a needed rest. The ascent was an even more painful rebirth out of depth and darkness into sunlight and space. Only the stringy flesh of the goat gave us strength to start. Roberto, our head muledriver who seldom drank, had become deathly sick from the tequila we had given the men the night before. He kept retching all morning; it was agony to watch him. All our legs were swollen with insect bites aggravated by sweat and dust. Even a rest at the orchards did us little good, for the mules had strayed off, forcing the drivers to hunt for them while the rest of us continued climbing on foot. When the drivers and their mules finally caught up with us late that afternoon, we were all played out and had climbed only halfway up before making camp at sundown near a Tarahumara village.

The Tarahumaras, primitive and shy and somehow embodying the softness and mystery of the Barranca itself, had allowed us but few quick glimpses of them on our way down. Their isolated huts and little corn *milpas* were always deserted, and we heard only the shrill, plaintive wail of their bamboo flutes warning of our approach. The sound seemed to have come a long, long way in space and time, as if from the mythical Humpbacked Flute Player depicted in prehistoric pictographs throughout all Indian America.

Bacajipara, as it was known, was not a village at all. Simply a pocket in the hills, a place-name around which loosely grouped, isolated families were living in rock huts or caves perhaps a mile apart, scraping tiny *milpas* of corn on steep hillsides strewn with great boulders, with a plough hewn from the crotch of a tree. Grinding the kernels on a stone *metate*. Tending a few goats and weaving the wool into belts, *serapes,* and *cobijas* on crude horizontal looms. A glance into a nearby hut revealed it all—the primitive life of a people, hiding from capture and forced labor centuries before, who had regressed to the cavern-womb of their eternal earthmother. They were still wary of our own presence and none of them was drawn to the light of our campfire. So before dawn we sent out our Tarahumara to invite them to call.

At sunrise they began to straggle into camp. Long before we could see them trudging over the hills we could hear, like a Penitente *pito,* the shrill whistle of their simple reed flutes, the *baka,* with its three holes for finger stops; and the hoarse beat of the small *tambor,* or drum, which they called a *kampora.* Unlike the solitary goat-herders in breechclout and headband we had glimpsed, they were dressed for the occasion. Barefoot women wearing voluminous skirts and red kerchiefs, all packing babies on their backs. Men in ragged pieces of trousers and shirts, more red kerchiefs tied around their throats, and with feathers stuck in their straw hats. Their approach was always the same. They would slither in softly on bare feet, eyes demurely lowered. Then they would raise both hands and gently touch their palms or the tips of their fingers to ours, sometimes murmuring a soft "Kevira," in greeting. Always this softness of voice, gesture, and manner. Then as they looked up, we could see in their black eyes the wild remoteness of the Barranca itself, the withdrawn look of a people who had not yet emerged from their dark depths; a pleading look, like that of an animal which begs the light of understanding.

There was little food left to give them: only what remained of the goat meat, beans, tortillas, and pots of strong black coffee sweetened with handsful of sugar. Gulping this down, they squatted in a circle, forty or more, to receive the little presents Rose gave them: cigarettes, matches, hand mirrors, needles and thread, safety pins, and lollipops and bubble gum, the first they had seen.

It was not much of a fiesta. The *baka* wailed plaintively, the *kampora* beat hoarsely. Somebody got out a hand-carved violin and began to squeak on it. One man and then another shuffled in a primitive dance among the rocks. The *Seligame,* their governor or chief, and the *Hechizero,* the medicine man or witch doctor, nodded approval. Their mere contact with strangers seemed rewarding enough.

Even at this great depth the sun finally cleared the rim of the canyon wall and touched the hollow with light. One could see the shadows in the people's eyes receding like the shadows of the cliffs. The coming of light! The miracle of every Emergence along man's continuing Road of Life. Yet these were a people who had never given in to its promise completely, who had never summoned the effort to break free from their eternal mother. Their dark eyes surrounding us in a great circle, eyes steady and fixed with a compelling wonder, still seemed to hold in their depths the perpetual darkness that lay like a pool on the floor of the Barranca.

The railroad stop above became our chief concern now. If we missed the train that afternoon, we would have to wait four days for the next one. So once again we resumed our slow climb upward with our patient, scrawny mules and faithful drivers. It struck me suddenly that our haste to catch the biweekly train was but a rational excuse. About our anxious ascent into sunlight there was a compulsion as great as our descent into darkness two days before. To shake off those cloying shadows; to rise into the light and freedom of full consciousness! This was the other great truth given me by this experience whose duration could not be measured in time, whose strangeness could not be forgotten. Long after the train whistled 'round the bend, and even months later, the look in the eyes of those Tarahumaras remained to stare at me over many a cup of midnight coffee. Yes! Man in his never-ending journey must return periodically to the depths of his arising. But he cannot remain there. He must keep on climbing toward the common destiny that awaits us all.

13. THE LOST WHITE BROTHER

During my last winter at Pumpkin Seed Point all the stresses and strains engendered by my long stay began to crack through the surface. Early one morning after a fresh fall of snow, White Bear in distress rushed over to me from the four-room, stone house that Brown Bear had bought. "She's kicked me out! We don't get any breakfast! There's no water!"

The evening before he had forgotten to fill the thermos jugs and bottles from the spring at Hotevilla. That morning when Brown Bear had got out of bed to draw water from the tap for coffee—it was not considered reliable enough to drink—nothing came out. The pipes were frozen. So Brown Bear, in a rage, had kicked him out.

After I had dressed, we went outside, jacked up my car in the snow to put on chains, and drove to Hotevilla for water. The pipe at the spring was frozen. There was another source not far away: the house of one of our informants, Bessie Sakmoisi, just outside the village of Bakavi. Bessie of the Side Corn Clan was a little dried-up woman of eighty who lived alone in her ramshackle hut. Becoming ill one night recently, she had dizzily wandered out in search of help and fallen off the cliff. That she survived was a miracle, but she was still unable to return to her isolated hut. In it, however, was a shallow well boasting a little, rusty handpump from which we could fill our water jugs.

Hardly had we turned off on the dirt road, now hidden by snow, than the car bogged down to the axles in a deep drift. There was no budging it. White Bear was obliged to trudge to Bakavi, bringing back a half-dozen Hopis with shovels to dig us out. Finally arriving at Bessie's house, we found the pump frozen solid. In despair we drove home, filling a jug at the trading post so we could have coffee. Brown Bear, still in a rage, refused to make it until we had thawed out the frozen water pipes in the house.

157

"Coffee! What do you want coffee for when there's no water for cooking, for washing, to work the toilet!" she stormed. "I'm sick of this crummy old house where nothing works! I'm tired of living on this damned Reservation with a bunch of lazy, shiftless Indians who don't have enough sense to come in out of the rain!"

So White Bear and I meekly went outside in the freezing cold, dug the pipes out of the frozen ground, and thawed them out over the stove inside the house. By the time we had wrapped them in rags and newspapers, and replaced them in the ground, it was mid-afternoon. Then, finally, we had coffee and something to eat.

Mystics and messiahs should be good plumbers.

Work on our project was coming to an end. White Bear was soon to be taken off the Foundation payroll, and Brown Bear was continually badgering him about the money she had wasted on it; an echo, it seemed to me, of government protests against expenditures for Indian projects.

She already had several new projects in mind. One of them, since she was sick of living on the Reservation, was to move to Sedona. Here she hoped to induce someone to build them a replica of a Hopi kiva which would also contain a souvenir shop. In the kiva White Bear would deliver lectures on Hopi religion to visiting tourists who would then file out into the souvenir shop to buy pieces of Hopi handicraft and copies of our published study which he would autograph as the authority on the subject. His reputation was already being established; a small pottery kiln was now using several of his little designs and symbols on the ashtrays it manufactured for sale at tourist souvenir shops. On the back of each was imprinted his signature: "White Bear, Expert on Hopi Religion."

If it often seemed to me that Brown Bear was too avid to exploit White Bear as a professional Indian for their own material gain, White Bear seemed tailored to fit the role of a Hopi messiah. His years of work on the project had not reconciled the conflicting aspects of his nature. They had intensified his obsessive belief in the literal meaning of Hopi myth. Yet the fallacy of his moving back into the hated white world which would soon be destroyed by his prophecied cataclysm, but to whose material comforts he had now become accustomed, was at once apparent. Of more concern to me was the fact that he was now beginning to project on me, as the Hopis long have projected on all whites, the image of a foreign intruder who had come to betray his people.

I realized this one evening when White Bear, sitting by the stove, said abruptly, "The true Pahana is coming soon."

"From where?" I asked quietly, remembering his relating once that the Hopis had confidently expected Nazi Germany to win the last World War and to befriend the Hopis because their insignia of the swastika was similar to the swastika symbol of the Hopi migrations. This hope seemed confirmed later when Japan entered the war as an ally of Germany, for its symbol of the rising sun was similar to the sacred sun symbol of the Hopis.

"It is not to be revealed yet," White Bear answered with portentous secrecy. "Maybe from the north and west. You white people will find out soon enough!"

Here it was again after our three years of intimacy: a strange, impersonal gulf across which I could not reach him. For an instant I felt him so alienated by the mytholological content of his own obsession that no other Hopi or white could reach him. In a little while I walked slowly back to Pumpkin Seed Point. Lying in bed, I kept wondering just what it was in that obsessive fantasy that separated White Bear and myself, that for so long had separated Indians and whites.

Pahana. That was the clue. The true Pahana from across

the great salt water—the lost white brother. Who was he, really?

The prophecied return of Quetzalcoatl, the white and bearded redeemer of the Toltecs and Aztecs, he who was known to the Mayas as Kukulcan, and to the Hopis as Pahana, was a myth of profound significance common to all Mesoamerica.

According to the Hopi version, their ancestors, upon their Emergence to this new Fourth World, were given four sacred tablets by the guardian spirit of the land. One of these tablets, inscribed with cryptic markings, had a piece broken off from one corner. Masaw, the guardian spirit, explained the meaning of the tablet and its strange markings.

The time would come after the people had migrated to their permanent home, he said, when they would be overcome by a strange people. They would be forced to develop their land and live according to the dictates of a new ruler or they would be treated as criminals and punished. But they were not to resist, warned Masaw. They were to wait for the person who would deliver them. This person was their lost white brother, Pahana (from *Pasu*—Salt Water), who would come with the people of the rising sun from across the great salt water with the missing corner of the sacred tablet, deliver them from their persecutors, and establish a new and universal brotherhood of man.

The Hopis did not forget this prophecy when they finally concluded their migrations. Every year in Oraibi, on the last day of Soyal, a line was drawn across a six-foot-long stick kept in the custody of the Bear Clan to mark the time for the arrival of Pahana with the people of the rising sun. The Hopis knew where to meet him too.

If he arrived on time, according to the prophecy, the Hopis were to receive him at the bottom of the trail leading up the east side of the mesa to Oraibi. If not, every five years thereafter they were to wait for him at points along the trail designated by prophecy: at Sikya'wa (Yellow Stone), Chekuwa (Pointed Rock), Nahoyungvasa (Cross Fields), and finally at Tawtoma (Where the Sunray Goes Over the Line to the Place) just below Oraibi, if he were twenty years late. Now the stick was filled with markings and the Hopis kept waiting for the predicted return of their redeemer, Pahana.

Far to the south in Mexico the return of the bearded, white god Quetzalcoatl was also anxiously awaited by the Aztecs. The myth of his arising, departure, and return was dear to every heart. Many centuries before he had appeared among the ancient Nahuatl people called Toltecs, "master artists." He came as a great king to lay the foundations of their culture. He discovered the maize which he gave to men; taught them to polish precious stones, to weave fabrics with cotton, to make bright-colored robes from the feathers of the quetzal; he taught the priests how to measure time from the movements of the stars, to institute ceremonies, and to fix the days for prayer and sacrifice. He was wise, good, and chaste.

Yet the day came when evil counselors induced him to get drunk and sleep with a woman, committing carnal sin. In anguish and penitence Quetzalcoatl abandoned his kingdom and immured himself in a stone coffin for four days. Then he went to the shore of the great sea, built a huge fire, and cast himself into the flames. For eight days now he remained underground in the Land of the Dead undergoing purification. Taking the form of a dog, he collected the bones of a man and a woman and sprinkled upon them his own blood. Thus he redeemed them in order that they could inhabit the earth. Eight days later he made his ascent, being transformed as the Lord of Dawn into the planet Venus, the Morning Star. Thereafter Venus astronomically repeated his ritual journey, first appearing in the western sky, disappearing underground for several days, then reappearing in the eastern sky to reunite with the sun.

Henriette Mertz offers proof that the bearded white god was a Buddhist priest named Hwui Shan who came from China in 458 A.D., his journey being recorded in one of the earliest Chinese Classics, Kuen 327, written in 499 A.D. during the Sung Dynasty. By her intuitive and painstaking translation Miss Mertz establishes with little doubt the results of his journey in both Mexico and China.

The hermetic quality of the myth that he engendered far transcended the limits of history and legend. As the perceptive archaeologist Laurette Sejourne points out, it was essentially the expression of the universal doctrine of sin and redemption; of death and resurrection; the transfiguration of man into god. To the analytical psychologist Erik Newmann, Quetzalcoatl was an archetype, a uniting symbol achieving the union of opposites: morning and evening star, heaven and earth, matter and spirit; and in resolving the problem of human duality and pointing the way of redemption for all men, he was the Redeemer.

That the Quetzalcoatl myth was profound and far reaching is at once apparent. Similar to Buddhism, and consolidating about the same time as Christianity, it spread to the far northern deserts and down into the Mayan jungles, dominating all Mesoamerica for more than a thousand years. If it is difficult for us today to accept its transcendental meaning, it was also difficult for the later Aztecs —and for the same reason. The Toltec culture was matriarchal, rooted in the unconscious; that of the Aztec patriarchal, reflecting the rise of consciousness with its male principle of light.

The Aztecs were warring tribes of crude Chichimecas, "barbarians," who about 1,000 A.D. began coming down into the Valley of Mexico from the north and overpowering the cultured Toltecs and their sacred City of the Gods, Teohihuacan. By 1325 A.D. the Aztecs had founded Tenochtitlan, now Mexico City, which soon became the capital of their vast empire: an empire whose facade was the resplendent Toltec culture, but whose transcendental religion was now distorted into a totalitarian cult of sun worship with its wholesale human sacrifices.

Yet from deep underground, from the hearts of men, kept welling the everlasting hope for the return of Quetzalcoatl, the redeemer, who would establish with his coming a new era of peace. As the year of his prophecied return approached—the year of Ce Acatl named for him—strange signs appeared to herald his coming.

There were eight of them, all omens of disaster. The first was a fire that appeared in the eastern sky, shaped like a flaming ear of corn. Then in swift succession the temple of Huitzilopochtli burst into flame and burned to the ground, followed by the destruction of the temple of Xiuhtecuhtli which was struck by a lightning bolt. The fourth wonder was comets flashing through the sky while the sun was shining. There were three of them, racing from the west to the east, shooting off sparks of fire and bright coals. The fifth portent came when the Lake of Mexico foamed and boiled with rage, destroying half the houses in Tenochtitlan. Soon this was followed by the voice of a weeping woman night after night, crying out in a loud voice, "O my children, we are lost! Where can I hide you?" The seventh omen was a strange bird resembling a crane that was trapped by fishermen in the lake. The bird wore in the crown of its head a strange mirror in which could be seen the *mamalhuaztli*, the three stars in the constellation Taurus. The eighth omen appeared on the streets of the city in the form of monstrous human beings with two heads. They were captured and taken to Emperor Moctezuma, but the moment he saw them they vanished.

In that year of Ce Acatl, 1519, Quetzalcoatl came. Hernan Cortés and his band of Spanish invaders landed on the east coast of Mexico. Native runners hastened to inform Moctezuma of their arrival. Their drawings and paintings on cotton cloth assured the Aztec ruler that the strangers were indeed the white and bearded gods accompanying Quetzalcoatl. He made haste to welcome them.

Five priests were sent to the coast. All five were garbed as gods. They carried with them the great plumed-serpent mask of Quetzalcoatl with which they arrayed Cortés, together with gifts that included a gold disc, big as a cartwheel, symbol of the sun; a great silver image of the moon; rich mantles; jewels; gold ornaments; perfumes; and flowers.

Escorted by these emissaries, and accompanied by hundreds of Tlaxcaltecan warriors, the little band of Spanish freebooters began their march inland to Tenochtitlan, capital of the Aztec empire.

On the way, writes Cortés, "I burned more than ten towns, of more than three thousand houses. . . . At dawn I fell upon a large town of more than twenty thousand dwellings. As I surprised them, they were unarmed. The women and children ran naked in the streets. And I fell upon them. . . ."

Reaching Cholula, sacred city of Quetzalcoatl, whose pyramid was larger than the Egyptian pyramid of Cheops, the Spaniards were received by priests and choruses of children singing and dancing, and feasted for two days. On the third day Cortés called all the inhabitants together. Priests, nobles, warriors, and populace crowded the great courtyard of the Temple of Quetzalcoatl, unarmed, with eager and happy faces, to hear what the fair god would say. The Spaniards attacked and killed them all—six thousand people in less than two hours "in a muck of intestines and blood."

Even so, the patient and forgiving Moctezuma welcomed them in Tenochtitlan, graciously asking why they had come. Cortés replied with the classic answer, "We are troubled with a disease of the heart for which gold is the only remedy."

Too late the Aztecs realized that the Spaniards were men, not gods. Moctezuma was killed by a stone thrown while he was remonstrating with his own people, and the siege of the island-city of Tenochtitlan began. Perhaps there is no story in all history as colorful and exciting, sad and repulsive, as the conquest of Mexico. That Cortés and his handful of 633 Spanish freebooters were able to level Tenochtitlan to the ground and destroy the greatest civilization in pre-Columbian America was not due solely to his courage and ruthless talent for intrigue and treachery. The Aztecs were betrayed by their own despotic rulers who, in order to control their subject tribes, had distorted the transcendental belief in Quetzalcoatl into a bloody, sacrificial cult of temporal power.

By 1533 it was all over; Cortés with the aid of rebellious other city-states had conquered the Aztec Empire, laid waste to the land, and won all Mexico for the crown of Spain. Seven years later Francisco Vasquez de Coronado with a resplendent company of *conquistadores* marched forth to extend the Conquest into the unknown wilderness to the north. Finding the seven golden cities of Cibola to be only the adobe villages of the Zuñi Indians, Coronado dispatched Pedro de Tovar with a small force to the so-called province of Tusayan which was said to contain seven more villages.

Here the Hopis were patiently awaiting the arrival of their own Redeemer and lost white brother, Pahana. By a strange coincidence the year of Quetzalcoatl's predicted arrival in Mexico, Ce Acatl, 1519, corresponded with the year Pahana was prophecied to come to the Hopis. As the bearded white gods were now twenty-one years late, all the Hopi clan and kiva chiefs met them at the last appointed rendezvous, Tawtoma, according to prophecy. Here four sacred lines of cornmeal had been drawn across the trail. The Bear Clan leader stepped up to the barrier and extended his hand, palm up, to the leader of the white gods, Tovar. If he were indeed the true Pahana, the Hopis knew he would extend his own hand, palm down, and clasp the Bear Chief's hand to form the *nakwach,* the ancient symbol of brotherhood.

Tovar instead curtly commanded one of his men to drop a gift in the Bear Chief's hand, believing that the Indian wanted a present of some kind. Instantly all the Hopi chiefs knew that the Pahana had forgotten the ancient agreement made between their peoples at the time of separation.

Nevertheless they escorted the Spaniards up the trail to Oraibi, fed and quartered them, and explained the ancient agreement. It was understood by this that when the two peoples were finally reconciled, each would correct the other's laws and faults, live side by side and share in common all the riches of the land, and join their faiths in one religion that would establish the truth of life in a spirit of universal brotherhood.

The Spaniards did not understand, nor were they able to produce the missing corner of the sacred tablet. The Hopis knew then that Tovar was not the true Pahana and that they could expect trouble. It came with more and more Spanish expeditions, the hated "Slave Church," tyranny and bloodshed; and these two centuries of Spanish rule were followed by another century under American domination.

Someday—and soon—it will be over. The Hopis still wait patiently for the true Pahana and the people of the rising sun.

We cannot underestimate the psychological significance of

this belief that has endured unshaken for more than fifteen centuries if only in the hearts of a remnant of a primitive people dwelling on the northern perimeter of a once great civilization. This ancient myth of pre-Columbian America still retains a profound meaning for us all. Pahana, like Quetzalcoatl and Kukulcan, is but another name for the "Being within, communing with past ages," as the Shawnee chief Tecumseh aptly called it—that universal Self whose manifestation is the unfulfilled longing of all humanity.

14. THE PAST REREAD

For the last time I walked back to the little house below Pumpkin Seed Point, lit the gas lamp, and crawled into bed. Our work was over. On the morrow I was going home to my little ranch a mile above the Spanish village of Arroyo Seco and adjoining the Taos Indian Reservation.

Home! How wild and beautiful it was! A thick-walled adobe set back of a stream in a lawn surrounded by great cottonwoods and flanked by a grove of aspens. Behind it a long hay rack and an adobe barn for my three horses. And stretching behind these into the pine-covered slopes of the Sangre de Cristos an apple orchard, a long field bordered by chokecherry and wild plum thickets, and backed by an untouched wilderness through which cut the Acequia Madre or Mother Ditch. It was nearly eight thousand feet high, and looking west you could see a seventy-mile stretch from the Colorado border to the gorge of the Rio Grande.

It would be Spring there. The wild plum blossoms against the pines would give the landscape the look of a Chinese print. The Indians cleaning out the irrigation ditches would have their cotton blankets wrapped around their heads like turbans and would be singing as they worked. Here at Pumpkin Seed Point all day towering yellow waves had been rolling in from the desert, breaking against the windows in sprays of stinging sand and powdery dust. That afternoon, to keep it from seeping through the cracks and covering every article in the room, I had spread rolls of wet newspapers along the door and window sills. This curious activity puzzled a group of half-naked Hopi children watching me outside. But then everything I had done here, months on end, had aroused the same earnest bewilderment. Shivering in winter cold or sweltering in summer heat, their noses were flattened every day against the pane. There was only one way to get rid of them. So I went out and distributed the last pieces from the candy jar, and came back to resume packing.

Now everything was ready. The bulky manuscript of text and drawings distilled from nearly three years' work was packed with my books in cartons brought from the trading post. My clothes were compressed in a suitcase and a bulky duffle bag. A few old kachinas had been taken down from the walls with a dozen willow branches to which were tied a multitude of prayer-feathers. These I would tie on the *vigas* in the house and barn at home. Among them was a magnificent eagle feather *paho* framed by a cornleaf, and tied with two tiny hawk feathers at the end of the quill by a handspun cord of native cotton of the prescribed length of a newborn rabbit—a parting gift of John Lansa. On the table sat a present from Paul Sewemaenewa, a huge and beautiful reed plaque whose central design was a symbol of his own Eagle Clan. Otto Pentiwa had carved me a kachina. There were more little presents from other friends.

How good it would be to leave these barren, parched Hopi mesas so aloof and lonely under their depressive miasma of defeat and decay! Yet as I lay there in bed I began to find it hard to leave Pumpkin Seed Point. Perhaps difficulties and disappointments endear a place more than beauty and pleasure. Or perhaps it was something I had left undone, a feeling of something yet unresolved. I wondered what it was.

Late that afternoon after packing I had walked down to the two Bears' house. Brown Bear's farewell dinner was a feast of our favorite Hopi dishes: the lamb and hominy stew known as *knukwivi,* baked corn, red, blue, and white piki, and a melon that had been preserved in sand all winter. It should have been a jolly celebration. We had spent a long time together, weathered all storms, and finished our study. Still the feeling persisted that something had come to an end without having been wholly resolved.

White Bear's attitude confirmed my uneasiness. During the past year he had given the Angel of Wall Street, the Foundation director, and myself great concern. We regarded him as a very shaky but necessary bridge which we hoped would not collapse before our work was finished. It had not collapsed and our work was done, but I was worried about him. He was now fully possessed by his archetype. Reality of course did not justify his assumption of the role of messiah for all his people or a spokesman for any group. A relative of his, Thomas Banyacya of New Oraibi, was now recognized as the official spokesman for the Hopi Independent Nation, as the Traditionalists now called themselves, indicating that White Bear's assumptions were ignored. Here on the Reservation he was still abnormally shy and retiring, not accepted as a member of any village group of Traditionalists, and still generally known as Oswald Fredericks. Only in the white world outside could he confidently assert himself as the Hopi prophet, White Bear. In any case, I doubted that our study, when published, would issue in a new era of peace throughout the Hopi mesas.

The thought, as I lay in bed, was not encouraging. If we ourselves had not been able to close the gap between us, how could the larger worlds of which we were a part? Yet whatever the status of Hopi politics, secular and religious, our study had thrown into historical focus the immemorial conflict between Indians and whites. The Indians, first seeing in us their lost white brothers who would establish the universal pattern of Creation, had then projected on us the causes of our mutual failure. We in turn projected on them our own fears of the mysterious spirit-of-place of the new continent and of the inimical forces of nature within us. So it was that we both, the red and the white, projected upon each other the repressed dark shadow of our dual nature, bringing forth the tragedy of America.

170

If our almost complete extermination of Indians set a precedent novel in history, it was a pattern of colonial conquest now out of fashion. Yet it seemed to me that we were still persisting in this projection of our un-understood selves. We whites seem unaware of the psychic and even anatomical changes that the secret forces of the land have worked in us, transforming us in a few genera.ʹ.ᴜᵣ into a people as distinctly American as the first children of its soil. Time and the development of consciousness have also worked their change upon the Indians. We both must recognize these inner changes that are slowly integrating tribes, races, and nations the world over by meeting each other on a new and higher level of perception.

Many years ago Jung visited my neighboring Indians of Taos Pueblo. He was so impressed that he related the occurrence in a talk given in 1929 before the Guild of Pastoral Psychology in London, in his autobiography, and in a letter to Miguel Serrano shortly before he died. In them he stated:

> "We are sorely in need of a Truth or a self-understanding similar to that of Ancient Egypt, which I have found still living with the Taos Pueblos. Their chief of ceremonies, old Ochiwiay Biano (Mountain Lake), said to me: "We are the people who live on the roof of the world, we are sons of the Sun, who is our father. We help him daily to rise and cross over the sky. We do this not only for ourselves, but for the Americans also. Therefore they should not interfere with our religion. But if they continue to do so (by missionaries) and hinder us, then they will see that in ten years the sun will rise no more.'
>
> "He correctly assumes that their day, their light, their consciousness, and their meaning will die, when destroyed

through the narrow-mindedness of American Rationalization, and the same will happen to the whole world, when subjected to such treatment."

Their light, their meaning, have not died in the four decades since the old chief spoke. The sun still rises, and it rises upon a minority white world fragmented and disintegrating under the monstrous materiality and stifling rationalization that has blocked the rise of its unconscious contents into consciousness. It rises upon the dark world of Africa, South America—on all Eurasia and Asia whose teeming populations are rising like an angry tide to obliterate forever, with the assertion of their own freed archetypes, the illusion of white supremacy and economic domination.

So in this great verge I see these solitary Hopi mesas rising out of the pelagic plain as islands rising offshore the great unknown continents within us all. Their people are not wholly submerged in the darkness nor yet fully exposed to the light, but waiting expectantly to receive us as did those who first met our forefathers on the shore of the Atlantic. Once more we must go to them, not as invaders despising them as primitive savages but as their lost white brothers, without prejudices and projections. This time their language will not be new to us. They speak intuitively to the heart with the appeal of the appallingly simple, and they speak in the idiom of an America which has shaped our own lives and thoughts.

What they tell us seems to come out of the earth itself. The very stones whisper their secrets and the great breathing mountains shout out the shapes of their thoughts. These are myths nurtured in archaic darkness long before the light of the Holy Grail illumined the hearts of Europe, and told in ancient walled cities long before the stones of Westminster Abbey were hewn. They tell of man's emergences from previous worlds, of the seven womb-caverns of the human soul, of the seven golden cities, of the dark eye of the animal kingdom, and of the prophecied coming of the redeemer. They tell of a land that is itself a living entity; of a great pool of time, motionless and fathomless, in which the plan of all Creation unfolds its petals at its own measureless pace. And suddenly all these myths lose for us their barbaric strangeness, their primitive cast. By the miracle of their truth and beauty, they remind us that we know them well.

Such are the riches that await our coming. But the red men must learn to recognize us by the missing corner of their sacred tablet which we bring—our rereading of their ancient myths. From it they will understand that universal truths cannot be preserved as the exclusive spiritual property of any one tribe or race. Each travels with all humanity the same Road of Life; no great cataclysm will destroy all the earth and its peoples save one dwindling group obsessed with a mythical sense of superiority. So we must meet again, not only the red and the white, but pragmatic and primitive men everywhere, if we are to achieve the great task of the future—the integration of instinct and reason upon the higher level of intuition.

So, as I turned out the flickering gaslight for the last time in the little house at Pumpkin Seed Point, I felt that my long stay among the Hopis had not been completely unrewarding after all. I had not met the full exactitudes of a true Pahana, but I had glimpsed what they must be. Signs and portents foretell, as clearly now as in Moctezuma's time, that this ancient planet Earth faces another hinging hour in the biography of mankind. We must heed them if we are to make of this end of a tragic era the beginning of a new age more fruitful for us all.

GLOSSARY

Selected list of Indian and Spanish/Mexican words used in this book

amole . . . . roots of soap-weed yucca
arriero . . . . muleteer
atole . . . . *pinole* boiled into a gruel
baka . . . . reed flute
barranca . . . . canyon
cobija . . . . blanket
concho . . . . faster
conquistador . . . . conqueror
cuidado . . . . look out!
dutuburi . . . . Tarahumara Indians' ceremonial dance
ferrocarril . . . . railroad
hechizero . . . . medicine man
hopi . . . . peace
jacal . . . . hut
javelina . . . . wild pig
kampora . . . . drum
kekelt . . . . fledgling hawk
kisonvi . . . . center of the village, plaza
kivaove . . . . the part above, the visible portion of a kiva
protruding above ground
knukwivi . . . . . . stew of lamb and hominy (customary Hopi meal)
kopavi . . . . open door, often the soft spot on top of one's head
koshare . . . . Pueblo Indian clown
manta . . . . cape, shawl
mercado . . . . market
metate . . . . curved stone for grinding (e.g. corn)
milpa . . . . small field of corn
mujer . . . . lady
mula . . . . mule

174

nakwach .... ancient Hopi symbol of brotherhood: horizontal clasped hands

ngakuyi ...... medicine-water: made from bones of wild animals (e.g., bear, mountain lion, wolf) ground and mixed with water

pahos .... prayer-feathers

paso .... juncture

piki ...... distinctive Hopi bread, made of finely ground cornmeal baked to a paper-thin cake (usually on a piece of tin), then rolled up to the size of a large sausage, crisp and delicately flavored, it comes in all the colors of Hopi corn: white, yellow, red, blue

pinole .... roasted and ground corn mixed with water

pito .... whistle, wail

posi .... medicine man

powaqa .... sorcerers, witches

puesivi .... caves

ramada .... mass of branches

ranchito .... camp

salavi .... spruce tree

seligame .... chief

serape .... shawl

sipapuni .... path from navel, place of man's Emergence from underworld

tambor .... drum

tamochpolo .... power to draw up the muscles back of the knee thus crippling a man

tesguino .... corn beer

tortilla .... flat corn pancake

tuhika .... medicine man

viga .... rafter, beam

visitas .... Christian missionary contacts

zaguan .... narrow alley